DEIRDRE & DAEDALUS:
No Ordinary Love
A Memoir

by
DEIRDRE L. HALL

Published by Lulu Publishing & Limelight Publishing.
Copyright © 2014 DEIRDRE L. HALL
All Rights Reserved.

All images ©1965-2020 Deirdre L. Hall
All Rights Reserved

This is a work of non-fiction. Except as provided by the Copyright Act no part of this publication may be reproduced, stored in a retrieval system or transmitted in any form or by any means without the prior written permission of the publisher.

Cover design @ Limelight Publishing.

Paperback: ISBN 978-0-9972577-0-0
Hardcover: ISBN 978-0-9972577-1-7
eBook: ISBN: 978-0-9972577-2-4

lulu.com
limelightpublishing.com

Contents

FOREWORD 1
PROLOGUE 3
Chapter *One* 9
Chapter *Two* 15
Chapter *Three* 25
Chapter *Four* 48
Chapter *Five* 56
Chapter *Six* 72
Chapter *Seven* 75
Chapter *Eight* 77
Chapter *Nine* 88
Chapter *Ten* 105
Chapter *Eleven* 113
Chapter *Twelve* 163
Chapter *Thirteen* 178
Chapter *Fourteen* 185
Chapter *Fifteen* 191
Chapter *Sixteen* 199
Chapter *Seventeen* 204
Chapter *Eighteen* 215
Chapter *Nineteen* 225
Chapter *Twenty* 234
Chapter *Twenty-One* 245
Chapter *Twenty-Two* 259
Chapter *Twenty-Three* 270
Chapter *Twenty-Four* 275

1992-2013	277
EPILOGUE	290
Music Lyrics Copyright Acknowledgments	297
NOL REFERENCE INDEX	302

Dedication

*For my Aunt, Alma J. Pearsall,
who left her indelible fingerprints on my life.
You are forever in my heart.*

Reader Content Warning

The chapters beyond this page contain disturbing and/or offensive material that might cause emotional distress.

Dear Reader, thank you for choosing this book. Please know that I always strive to be sensitive and walk through the world with mindfulness, especially for those that have survived a traumatic experience. For that reason, I am putting the choice in your hands to decide how to engage with the possible triggering content.

[Deirdre](#) & Daedalus: No Ordinary Love by Deirdre L. Hall (abuse; emotional abuse, verbal abuse, physical abuse, absent parent, abusive relationship, domestic abuse, alcoholism, bullying, death, murder, depression, drugs, homophobia, hospitalization, loss of a loved one, medical language, pregnancy, abortion, rape, sexual assault, sexual violence, suicidal thoughts, terminal illness, trauma, PTSD)

FOREWORD

Deirdre & Daedalus: No Ordinary Love

She walks in a room; the sun shines. Her eyes speak without saying a word; they greet you with warmth and love like you have known her all your life. To know Deirdre L. Hall is to love her—and I love her. Her infectious personality allows you to let go and follow her to friendship. When we found each other on Facebook, the heavens opened up. We were best friends in High School, LaGuardia Fiorello Music & Art High School, the school "Fame" where friends are made, and creativity lives. From 1980-1984, our lives intertwined with music, boys, and dreams of success. Fast-forward to 2015, and we are still talking about music, the good men in our lives and success; but on a womanhood level.

When Deirdre asked me to read her manuscript Deirdre & Daedalus: No Ordinary Love, I was honored. I read her story at night when the moon was high, and silence cloaked the air. The words jumped off the pages and came to life—they invited me in to be a part of the journey. I was a welcomed stranger in Deirdre's musical narrative of sharps and flats filled with love & happiness; love & heartbreak; love & forgiveness; love & resilience; love & triumph; and love & love again.

When you read the pages, you will be swept in as I was, and you won't want to leave.

Deirdre will take you on a voyage of the ups and downs of her life funneled through her writing journal, which is the center of the story. Hall uses her chronicles to weave you into the intricacies of her relationships with her parents, her music, and Daedalus. Daedalus, the one who would take her to the heavens and back. There are times when you'll scream at one page and cry and laugh at another. As you travel with Deirdre through the chronicles of her life, you will find a girl who became a woman by trial and error, who went through the valley but came out shining. Deirdre survives through her music and the power of the pen. You feel the music throughout the memoir, and you are rooting for her to win in life and love.

Deirdre is an extraordinary writer, actor, musician, and human being. Her sensitive account of sharing her life is, at the core, a love story. Deirdre & Daedalus: No Ordinary Love is an honest, inspiring and heartfelt look at life and the lessons of love. I am sure that all who read it will see and feel the compassion and honesty of her words, her songs, and her life.

The multiple gifts inside of Deirdre L. Hall cannot be contained . . . she must fly.

February 5, 2015
Michele Sweeting-DeCaro
Adjunct Professor, City College of New York, Center for Worker Education

PROLOGUE

Ok! Here I am! Standing before you. Feeling naked and vulnerable. Why? Because I've been thinking about writing this story for a long time now. Actually decades.

First, the honest truth is that it took me this long because at first glance it seemed so audacious of me to think that anyone in the world would want to read about my life. Secondly, no matter what I said or how I said it, some people would feel hurt or embarrassed with me adding them into my story as supporting cast members or as a side character. Because truth be told, everyone wants to be the hero of their own life story and they always want to be seen in the best light possible, right?

However reluctant I was to risk the backlash, I decided that I was unwilling to delete all the untidy but rich material in order to sanitize the story just to convey a flattering account. Moreover, I did not want to be judged. But the need to speak my truth compelled me and far outweighed the fears.

In writing this story, my story, our story, it allows me to finally share it with you and the world. And so anyone who dares feel the need to judge me, well then I say "plague on all your houses!" It is my deliberate intention to stay true to my story. In doing so it is my hope that in me revealing experiences in my life and illuminating my humanity to others, they too will feel safe, free and confident enough to equally reveal their humanness universally.

My objective is to be authentic, for my own sake; for the sake of Daedalus; for the sake of truth; for posterity. Please know that in reading this, I'm not writing this story from what I think or imagined happened. This story is taken word for word from the pages of my journal.

As someone who's always kept a journal, over the years I have always set aside time, albeit the early morning hours or at the end of the day, to write about what was going on in my life. Writing as with singing and acting has always been another natural form of self-expression for me. In keeping a journal, it always gave me a place to work out my problems, allowing me to think things through on paper. It was a safe space where I could get out my pent-up emotions, and express feelings and opinions that I didn't feel comfortable talking about to other people.

It doesn't get easier re-living this particular pivotal moment in time again but now it will be out loud instead of replaying it over and over in my head, re-reading it in the pages of my diary or having these memories echoing in every beat of my heart.

Although some of these memories were and are at times today still painful, from where I stand on this day, I have come to appreciate the young woman that I was then and how I've grown more into myself over the years. Funny, there are still days when I internally feel like that young, girlish, people pleasing twenty-year-old who wanted to have great adventures, see the world, express her passion on stage and live life to the fullest. A vibrant, fresh faced romantic who wanted a great partner who loved, cherished and adored her. Someone who shared her same values and would eventually have a family of her own.

Well, I've been fortunate enough to travel some, perform on various stages in theatre and countless other venues with my bands. I've gone up two dress sizes, okay maybe three dress sizes. I still have tons of energy and haven't lost my curious nature and love of learning.

I've had amazing adventures with some remarkably interesting people in some unusual places. Some of which would make you blush. Out of all the relationships I've had; not that I've had many, I've been fortunate in this life time to be able to call two of them the great loves of my life.

I am no longer a people pleaser, and don't really give a damn about what people think of me. My goal is staying in alignment with who I am at my core, and remaining in a place of peace and happiness no matter what's going on in the world or in my life. Sometimes when I look at myself in the mirror, if I look close enough, my eyes are tinged with a bit of sadness that comes with living life and dealing with loss but my sparkle and vivacity is still there.

In sharing this story, my story, I get to revisit my younger self but come back to her with empathy, non-judgment and a clearer understanding of just how free, trusting, accepting, loving, courageous, compassionate and resilient she was and I really am and how fearless, kindhearted and confident I have grown. While I'm constantly evolving and yes, can be quite entertaining, outgoing and social, sometimes can be a bit exasperating to family and friends. Yet, at my core I still am and probably will forever remain that creative, introverted, introspective, quiet, shy girl who was and is extremely sensitive. I still love life and all the possibilities that it has to hold for me. I love the theatre, music and singing, writing and the arts as passionately as ever. Perhaps even more so now that I've had the chance to live life a little. Nevertheless, I still have a longing to make my mark in this world. I don't have children so there won't be a child of mine to carry on my legacy or to tell my story. I guess when all is said and done, I just want the world, somebody to know that I was here. That I had something to bring to the table. That I was able to encourage at least one person to live in their truth. That I was able to bring a little light into the world.

Born from my resilience I have found and become at peace with who I am. My mistakes have humbled me along the way and because of my life experiences; they have helped me accept my vulnerability.

Even though I am perfectly imperfect I try not to let my inadequacies hinder me. However, we all know it's easier said than done right? Nowadays, I don't believe failing at something is necessarily failure. It took me a while to get that. Yet there were times when I had perceived I had failed in some major way and it caused me to struggle immensely with negative thoughts of not being enough. Some of those thoughts were so dark and twisty that I had even contemplated suicide a few times in my life.

But see here's the thing with us resilient folk; we possess enough self-awareness to know that negative thinking and destructive actions are eventually counterproductive and can be detrimental to our health. Over the years I've had setbacks just like anyone else and some of those stumbling blocks took me a while to bounce back from. How did I combat some of these obstacles? Well, church was a refuge for me when I used to practice Christianity. Some of my healing also involved meditation, healing crystals, reading, psychotherapy, medication, music, spiritual guidance and by way of my own moxie.

What I know for sure is that finding my inner strength wasn't about blind optimism or looking only on the bright side of life or stifling down negative emotions. It's about doing the work. It's truly about letting myself experience what I feel in any given situation, whether it's good or bad. I'm not about covering over my negative emotions; which is something my family is really good at by the way. Instead, I let my negative emotions sit side by side and marinate with indifference with my other feelings.

I am always mindful of being compassionate with myself. No judgments. Shit happens! No matter how you slice it, it's an inescapable fact of life.

So, the gist of it is that I wrote Deirdre & Daedalus: No Ordinary Love to find my voice. To find beauty and purpose in the pain and grief of my experiences. To know and declare to the world that love is possible and lasting and real.

With that said…

Chapter *One*

Papa loved to love me
Nobody tried to save me
Papa loved to love me
Now I'm the one who's crazy…-Ledisi
"Papa Loved to Love Me", ©- LeSun Records

I didn't have the most auspicious start in life. Let's just say that being a child conceived from rape is a hell of a way for any human being to be starting out in the world.

For my mother, being a victim of rape had to be one of the most traumatic events she has had to experience and carry. No one should ever have to be exposed to this. I know this is a heavy subject and I must admit that I have to take a deep breath right now to settle the agitation in my stomach. Riddle me this? Why is it that no one ever talks about Children Conceived from Rape (CCR)? For a child conceived in rape, identity can be an internal, never-ending battle and this conflict can cast a lifelong shadow over our lives. I know! Living such a heavy legacy of this magnitude from such a disgusting and vicious crime is so unconscionable to many of us.

Nevertheless, I've continued to live it and in doing so come to know just how strong I really am. I can unequivocally say that part of my fortitude comes from the strong women in my family. Most notably, my mother who in spite of her difficult life, to this day is one of the most warmhearted, benevolent, kind, and honorable human beings that I have ever known.

First, let me be clear that as a young girl and as a grown woman I have always been, and always will be a never wavering pro-choice advocate. I think it's fucking outrageous that after forty-one years the Roe v. Wade decision on legalized abortion regarding children who were conceived through rape versus women who were raped and chose to end the pregnancy, at present is still aggressively being debated, opening a new front in the often intense discussions of a decades old culture war.

There was a young man who briefly became the poster child for the pro-lifer groups by the name of Ryan Bomberger. Ryan is a passionate pro-life advocate whose mother had been raped at the age of fifteen years old and she put him up for adoption.

Ryan has been quoted as saying "I was a product of rape BUT I was so loved that it never became an issue for me that I was a creation of rape." From articles that I've read it appears that Ryan has gone through life unfazed that he is a CCR. Ryan and I do in fact have some things in common. My mother was also raped at the age of fifteen, and my mother so loved me that she gave me life and chose to raise me on her own. Listen, I'm glad that I've had a full life too but here is where Ryan and I differ.

Can we please, if just for a moment shift our focus from the women of this violent crime of rape and incest and focus on the mental health of the children that are born? You see, no one ever really discusses the big picture of what happens emotionally, psychologically and mentally to children conceived from rape. Well let me tell you, we struggle.

We fight internally with ourselves and with the continuous litany of "what ifs." What if we possess the same DNA of the criminal? What if we are permanently seen as a representation of the unfathomable trauma inflicted on our mother?

What if that maliciousness was embedded in my genetic makeup? What if people can tell, somehow, that I had been created from violence? What if I went on to have a son, would he be a rapist, too? We are all well aware that survivors of rape face challenges with intimacy, anxiety, depression, insomnia and Post-Traumatic Stress Disorder because it is well documented and articulated on television, in books, psychological studies, film and even in our music. Take a listen to Ledisi's "Papa Loved to Love Me" from her Soul Singer album.

But what really pisses me off are the neoconservatives, tea- party republicans and pro-life organizations who tuck their prejudices, hate and judgments inside their bibles and vomit their hateful opinions onto others under the guise of religion. I find it offensive and insulting to my humanity.

Republican candidate for U.S. Senate, Representative Todd Akin of Missouri proclaimed that pregnancy rarely occurs as a result of what he calls "legitimate rape." Why? Because the female body has a way to shut its own reproductive system down so she can't become pregnant by being raped.

First, what the fuck is a legitimate rape? Can rape really be sincere and genuine?

Oh, and let's not forget his playmate, Indiana State Treasurer and U.S. Senate nominee Richard Mourdock, whose view on women who are raped stated that "life was something that God intended even if the pregnancy was due to rape."

His proclamation thereby confirms for me that he believes that forcing women who have become pregnant from rape or incest or to force any rape victim to carry the child to term is perfectly acceptable. That it's a "gift from GOD" is for me one of the most disturbing and difficult aspects of the entire abortion debate.

See, its declarations like these under the pretense of Christianity that are some of the reasons that I left the church long ago and would never be a part of a church again.

Musician, Singer and Artist, Meshell N'degeocello has a song titled "The Way" that I use to perform with my band years ago which spoke to me when I was considering Buddhism at the time. I felt it was a piece of philosophical prose that pretty much summed up for me the hypocrisy of Christianity. *"...Maybe Judas WAS the better man, and Mary made a virgin just to "save face". I too am so ashamed on my bended knees praying to my pretty white Jesus. They say you're the way, the light, the light so blinding. Am I not to question? Your followers condemn me. Your words are used to enslave me..." (Meshell N'degeocello© Warner/Chappell Music, Inc.)*

Ugh, the pure deception of right to lifers and the GOP sickens me. We are all cognizant of the fact that rape victims are more often than not made to feel like the rape was their fault. But for a lot of us CCR survivors we spend the entirety of our lives learning to cope with "their" supposed mistake. Because of the psychological and emotional toll this trauma has on us, some of us continue to put ourselves in abusive situations over and over because we have been bullied for questioning the truth of our existence and our experiences which in turn causes us to always doubt ourselves.

While in the process of doing a lot of work on myself, I realized that we are only as sick as the secrets we keep.

When I finally got to therapy at the age of about twenty-two, my Therapist confirmed what I had instinctively known. Once your secrets are spoken aloud, even if to just one person, they lose their power. Each time I acknowledged them, looked at them, felt them, I began to no longer feel the shame that kept me silent.

Yes, I could have written this part of my story years ago, and in hindsight I probably should have but here I am now putting it in print, adding my voice to the millions of others and finally pulling back the curtain from a dark moment in my life and all of us survivors.

My prayer to the world is to please understand that for children conceived in rape, these difficulties are magnified and leave everlasting wounds seen and unseen, especially if knowledge of our conception was shrouded in secrecy as in my case. Yes, some of us feel tormented by the knowledge that our conception was the absolute antithesis of what was desired. At best, it was a mistake. We were a mistake. At worst, a brutal crime was committed against our parent.

Look, I'm not trying to convert anyone. I am pro-choice! I am pro-choice because I believe that whether a pregnancy was the result of rape, or a pregnancy was very much not wanted or because of a dire medical circumstance the person could not carry the pregnancy to term, my stance is that it's not for the government or a religious faction to decide for us. For me, no matter what religious affiliation you are, we should not judge. It should always be a woman's personal right to choose for herself or along with her husband or partner what's best for her and her family.

You know, I have often pondered whether or not I would have made the same decision my mother did in carrying a child conceived from rape to full term and raise that child.

Ambivalent about it over the years, today I honestly don't think I would have made the same choice as my mother. I would have terminated the pregnancy. Nevertheless, the dire circumstance would have been that I would not exist. All the same, at this instance, the violent conditions and the people involved in how I came to be in this world will be left for another story at another time.

Chapter *Two*

Manic voices dressed like Hollywood pimps living in suburbia
Searching for things forbidden
They're in search, in search of lost connections
The voices inside my head- Deirdre L. Hall "Voices"- Deirdre L. Hall
©Red-Ride Music LLC.

Now as a performer I have been in front of the camera as a model, as an actor on stage in theater and television, a singer, percussionist and spoken word artist. And while these jobs have been fun and amazing there was always lots of time spent back stage waiting for your next scene, wardrobe, make-up or set changes, lighting fixes, and script re-writes. While having so much time on my hands during these moments, I was either caught up in deep conversations about life or playing spades with cast members, working on monologues or having fun acting a fool.

In my quiet moments spent putting on make-up or getting into character I would often contemplate with amusement how certain aspects of my life would have made for a grand Shakespearean play.

For instance, how ironic is it to have such a strong affinity and passion of music, knowing that you want to sing and be a performer but as a child be diagnosed with Otosclerosis. Otosclerosis is a disorder that causes progressive deafness due to overgrowth of bone in the inner ear. Most often initiated when one of the bones in the middle ear, the stapes, becomes stuck in place. When this bone is unable to vibrate, sound is unable to travel through the ear and hearing becomes impaired.

Over the years I have had three surgeries to correct my hearing loss. My first surgery on my right ear at the age of twelve years old in Chapel Hill hospital in North Carolina where they did an exploratory stapedectomy. The second surgery was in my mid 20's, was again on my right ear to fix a perforated ear drum caused from the piece of metal placed in my ear from my original surgery in North Carolina in addition to correcting the 20% hearing loss. During my early 30's, my final surgery was on my left ear where I had experienced a 30% hearing loss. Shout out to my wonderful ENT doctor Geoffrey Pollack in NYC.

There were very real dangers to having these surgeries. There was a slight chance of permanent hearing loss. There could be constant dizziness or facial paralysis. I remember doctor Pollack explaining to me that the nerve that assists the muscles of the face runs through the ear. Therefore, there was a slight chance of paralysis in the movement of my facial muscles for closing my eyes, making a smile and raising my forehead which could be partially or completely paralyzed and may well happen immediately after surgery or as a delayed onset.

Scared shitless and feeling the fear take my entire body hostage, he proceeded to inform me I may possibly have Tinnitus; ringing in the ear or also have taste abnormalities because of the small nerve that runs through the ear is also responsible for delivering some of the taste and salivary functions. After my ear surgeries, I did experience a bit of dizziness and an abnormal taste buds but the problems improved over time. The risks were pretty scary to me, but the thought of never being able to sing or listen to music was even scarier. Not being able to express myself through music would have been an unendurable tragedy.

Think about it. The essence of Shakespeare's tragedies is for the most part the expression of one life's in all of its abundant contradictions. Over the years I've come to name them my "paradox of disillusionment" just for kicks. Some of my misfortune and obstacles created dreadful experiences but were in fact brilliant in hindsight because they actually ended up producing creative and enchanting experiences in my life in so many other ways.

Now, my life's disappointments shine through me by way of grace and laughter. My resilience was shaped out of my ability to embrace innumerable, serious, life-changing situations. I found courage in my ability to walk through the fire and handle the setbacks as they occurred. There were plenty of people, conditions or opportunities that I thought I wanted. I strived hard to make them happen but once I got them, I became dissatisfied; discovering that the things or circumstances were not good for me or wasn't as amazing as what I imagined they would be. Thus, the paradox of my disillusionment.

Sir Shakespeare's works of art are all about setbacks, right? Crushed hopes and dreams and that an untimely death will face us all as human beings no matter who we are or where we come from. Traumatic life events, hey, are very, very real and yet somehow, I think we share the intuitive feeling that they are often times out of place, not really meant to happen to us.

Distressing events; don't they seem to be like trespassers into our lives? At times this is what it felt like to me. Sigh. I know that tragic literature is often meant to confront us human beings over and over again with life's absurdities. Sometimes we can even become captivated by these provocations which leads me to believe why some people thrive on having drama in their lives. But damn it! There were times that I was so over having to confront myself and the absurdities of my life. However, confront them I did.

While working at a local New York television station, one chilly fall afternoon, while on my lunch break, I sat in the park crying my eyes out. A month prior I had come to the realization that I wanted to have a baby, be a mom with my then fiancé. We had been dating for a few years. While on the road on tour with a theatre company we got engaged, adding another few years of travelling, trying to set a date to get married, my baby fever kicked in. Eight years in, the love of my life decided that he didn't want children, ever, but forgot to tell me. I was confused and totally devastated with this news. After all, didn't we joke around about how perfect our kids would be and how we were going to take them on tour with us, dragging them into the studio and the theatre. I had given him all of me and my good baby making years and he broke my heart. Me, not knowing what to do with all these feelings of sadness swirling around inside, I became depressed and I shut down. There were no words to express the loss and betrayal I felt. Looking back on it now, perhaps I should have communicated to him better the pain I felt but at the time it was all I could do. I was paralyzed with anger, fear and sadness. At him and at myself. I felt that I wasn't enough. Why wasn't I good enough to marry or for that matter good enough to have a child with?

On top of that was the distressing decision I had to make about attending my upcoming family reunion. I was torn and struggled with my choice to be there because I would have to see and be in the presence of the family member that molested me at the age of nine when my brother and I lived in North Carolina with my grandparents for a couple of years. I wanted to see my family but I didn't want to see HIM. Little by little I stopped singing, writing and performing. I began isolating myself and obsessing on the things that happened to me in my past. I was consumed by my bleak future with my then beloved and became fixated on missing Daedalus. Melancholia set in. This began what I now lovingly call my "blue period." Many creative, artistic people have had them you know. Perhaps you've had one of your own.

Do you know that the association between mental health and artistic creativity has long been a subject of debate? Some of the world's most prominent and celebrated artists in history have created art and music that was a manifestation of the darkness of their depression.

Countless illustrators, writers, painters, sculptors and great musicians like jazz musicians and composers, Miles Davis and Thelonious Monk, Singer-songwriter and musician Rickie Lee Jones. American Cartoonist Charles Schultz of the great Charlie Brown characters suffered from clinical depression. Writer Jack Kerouac, synonymous with the 1950's Beat Generation, Michelangelo, sculptor and painter was bi-polar and also affected by depression. Even Pablo Picasso had a blue period.

In Picasso's "Blue Period" (1901-1904), his blue paintings depicted an array of destitute human beings. It's my understanding that he chose the color blue deliberately because for him it represented the abysmal, the coldness, signifying misery and despair which was used to exaggerate the hopelessness of the people portrayed, such as beggars, prostitutes, the blind, out-of-work actors and circus performers, as well as Picasso himself and his impoverished artistic friends. At the time, Picasso even wore blue clothes.

Now I was too much of a Fashionista to be reduced to only wearing the color blue or black for that matter. But when the melancholy set in, even the smallest tasks became overwhelming. I felt hopeless, unwanted, unloved, misunderstood, betrayed, strung along, fearful, and paranoid. I cried and cried; at work in the office, at work in the bathroom, on the subway and at home. That's all I seemed to do at that time was weep. My relationship, my anticipation of getting married to the man I so loved and finally having a family with was not going to happen. It was surreal to know that after the loss of Daedalus, the very things I had wished and hoped for as a new beginning for me, for my life, was unravelling.

Morning, noon and night I cried. I felt like the Pig Pen character in Charlie Brown with the dirty, dark cloud following me around everywhere. There was a lot going on in my life at that time, decisions I had to make that I didn't want to confront. I was so unhappy. I had lost my joy, my optimistic outlook on life and felt doomed. My trust was shattered. I felt I couldn't trust the people who said they cared for me and loved me. More importantly I lost trust in myself. How could I have been so blind? How could I have loved so hard and put my faith in someone who made me feel inadequate. Even my intuitive self was silent. I was alone. It felt like my world was falling apart. What was the point of being on this planet feeling like this, I kept asking myself?

One day at work, I answered the phone in tears. The random caller on the other end asked me if I was okay, should they call someone for me? I gave an almost inaudible "no I'm okay." I thought, this is really bad. I'm falling apart at work. I had become a shadow of my former self. I needed to get help before I did something drastic to try and relieve the pain I was in.

On this sunny yet brisk fall day while out for lunch I went to the park, sat on that park bench and decided to call the suicide hotline. Someone did in fact pick up and guess what? Do you know they asked me to hold? They put me on hold and with shitty elevator music playing. So here I am contemplating taking my life, reaching out for help and I'm placed on hold! This cracks me up every time I think about it, now. How's that for the absurdity of life!

After being placed on hold for what seemed like forever, feeling insignificant I hung up. I knew what I had to do.

I went back to work and put in for a few vacation days. I booked a hotel room and took a bus to Atlantic City. When I arrived, my room wasn't ready yet so I went into the casino and wandered around, observing people as they sat at the slot machines with their drinks and cigarettes. It was my feeble attempt at trying to feel connected to humanity but I felt nothing. My emotional state was precariously perched upon a sheer rock cliff. Overlooking the cliff was this great crevasse which was my future. My future, my life was a crater so deep that I couldn't see to the bottom of it. I was alone on one side of the chasm, looking to the other side. Feeling like there was no way I was going to safely make it to the other side alive and whole. On that other side, people in the casino were talking to one another, laughing and appearing to have a good time. I felt totally excluded and felt that there was no way to get to the other side of the abyss.

Finally, I got into my room, unpacked my overnight bag, sat my bottle of pills on the night stand, took a long hot shower and wrote my good bye letters to family and friends trying to explain why I was taking my life. In the middle of putting my goodbyes down on paper I got my period. Damn it, this was the second time this month and I had no tampons.

The Guardian Angel that was assigned to protect me in all things appeared in the form of the cashier at the local CVS down the street from my hotel. My eyes noticeably puffy from crying, the cashier asked me if everything was okay. He said, "Ms. whatever it is that you're going through please know that you will be okay, whatever it is things will get better. Get some sleep and things will look better in the morning." I did take some of those pills and lived to tell.

Great thing is, out of adversity comes creativity. I wrote a song about that day in the park; "Thine Own Self Be True". Here are the verses and chorus. To hear it in its entirety find me on line and take a listen.

A year ago my life collapsed,
Thought it was over and perhaps
It would be best for me to go.
Sat in the park, broke down and cried,
Could not hold on, I couldn't fight
Nothing left but just my shadow.

I didn't know
the person staring back at me in the mirror.
I had to let him go
he did everything he could to break my spirit.
I gave my SELF away,

No Ordinary Love

didn't think about the cost.
What a heavy price to pay.
Then a voice inside me said,
what I always knew.
To thine own self be true.
All your lies and your deceit
Ooo boy you knocked me off my feet
You turned me inside out
I couldn't tell my up from down
I loved you more than I did myself
I loved you more than life itself
I can't remember- when I gave up
My pride, my joy.

I didn't know
The person staring back at me in the mirror.
I had to let him go
He did everything he could to break my spirit.
I gave my SELF away,
Didn't think about the cost.
What a heavy price to pay.
Then a voice inside me said,
What I always knew.
To thine own self be true.

The roads I've traveled have been rough
Some lessons learned
I've had enough
And still I'm trying to find my way
The pain is gone – Yes I've made it through
I found the girl that I once knew
And here I stand to see another day

Yes I love
That person starring back in the mirror
I won't ever let her go
Her reflection is so much clearer
Never give yourself away
Listen to that voice it will guide your way
It will whisper softly to you, softly to you What I always knew
To thine own self be true -Deirdre L. Hall
"Thine Own Self Be True- Deirdre L. Hall-"©Red-Ride Music LLC.

Chapter *Three*

*...She's a girl that can't be beat.
Born and raised on ghetto streets.
She's a devastating beauty
a pretty girl with ebony eyes.-Stevie Wonder
"Ebony Eyes"-Jobete Music Co. Inc.*

Over the years I have grown to understand and believe that certain difficulties, challenges and traumatic experiences write on the slate of who I am but is not all that I am. Yes, I was conceived in a very brutal and violent environment but I am so much more than that. Yes, I came into a world amid chaos, laced with inhumaneness and violence and perhaps this is one reason why I strive for peace within and harmony around me. I'm forever grateful that I still have the capacity to love.

Let's see, what was going on in the world when I decide to make my entrance into it? Hmmm, the first US combat troops arrive in Vietnam and by the end of the year, 190,000 American soldiers are in Vietnam fighting in a war we should have never been in. Reverend Dr. Martin Luther King, Jr., and more than 2,600 others are arrested in Selma, Alabama, during demonstrations against voter-registration rules, which ironically and sadly we are still fighting today.

Our black-nationalist leader Malcom X was shot to death at a rally in Harlem. Black people had been rioting for six days straight in the Watts section of Los Angeles with 34 people dead, over 1,000 injured and nearly 4,000 people are arrested. President Johnson gets the Voting Rights Act of 1965 passed quickly in response to the violent events on the Edmund Pettus Bridge in Selma, Alabama also known as Bloody Sunday.

When I decide to show up in my physical form, the Academy Award went to My Fair Lady for Best Picture. Grammy Awards went to "The Girl from Ipanema" for Best Song and "Hello, Dolly" for Best Album. In the fall on 1965, the number one hit song in the U.S. on the day of my birth was "I Hear a Symphony" by The Supremes as compiled by Billboard Hot 100 (November 14 to 27, 1965). For some reason knowing that this was the number one song at the time of my birth has always felt good to me but I could never figure out why. Could it be the divine source energy within me, my soul or higher self's way of welcoming me into the crazy, chaotic, world? Perhaps it was music's way of choosing me. Ha, I know, I can see all the eye rolls and hear the teeth sucking right now. I'm reaching right? Okay, okay!

I was born to a 5'3 beautiful yet naïve sixteen-year-old, pecan colored, southern girl on the crisp Wednesday evening of November 24th in 1965. I arrived at 7:15pm, weighing in at 7 pounds, 4 ounces and was 19 ½ inches long.

My mother was born in Mount Olive, North Carolina to Bessie Mae. Bessie was the eldest of 12 siblings whom she ended up having to raise because her own mother had died.

Miss Bessie Mae as people lovingly addressed her was a domestic worker for a white lady named Ms. Griffith and her family during the week. My mother's father Hardy, a gentle and kind man was a farmer who had previously joined the United States Army when he came of age. They had three children together. They ended up divorced because long story short, Bessie Mae didn't want to be a farmer's wife.

Word on the street was that she was "fast" meaning she loved partying and having a good time and gave the impression that she was easy. Bessie also had a thing about juke joints and couldn't stay out of the popular ones in the town. When my grandmother left him, she also left her three children behind. My uncle left my grandfather Hardy's farm and joined the military as soon as he could. My mom and aunt were still there and then for some reason my grandmother brought my mother and aunt back to live with her and her new husband leaving my granddaddy Hardy all alone.

Elders in my family have said that my granddad Hardy died of a broken heart. The doctors said it was Emphysema. I was about seven years old when he passed. We later found out that while we thought during the 1960's they had legally split; my grandmother was in fact a bigamist. She didn't actually divorce my grandfather until after her second husband G. Smith died.

My grandmother had remarried to this character named G. Smith who she had met in town partying. To this day a couple of the children my grandmother had with G. Smith actually have the last name from her first husband, my granddad Hardy on their birth certificates. When her second set of children were born, she hadn't officially divorced Hardy. The Smith boys found this out when they joined the military and their last names on their birth certificates did not have their biological father's name. What a mess!

    Not one to understand her motives but for some reason my grandmother was always apathetic when it came to my mother. So much so that she allowed her second husband G. Smith, who I grew up also calling him grandfather, raped my mother at the age of 15. Let that sink in for a moment.

    So, the man who I thought was my grandfather and ALL of my family led me to believe that it was so, was in fact my biological parent. My biological father was a rapist and my grandmother chose to build a life and family with a man who was brutal and violent. Therefore, every summer vacation, every family reunion was based on lie. I wasn't visiting my grandfather and my aunts and uncles. I was spending time with my bio father along with my half siblings who are also half brothers and sisters to my mom as well. I found this out by accident from a big mouth relative who let it slip and confronted my mother about it when I was 15 years old.

    Like I said, my family was so very good at keeping secrets and not living in the truth. Sometimes truths can be uncomfortable, both for you and for other people, but this need not be the reason not to speak those truths. It is astonishing how often the harshest truths are also the most valuable. So perhaps you can understand why I dislike bull-shitting people and why honesty is so very important to me. I digressed. Again, another story for another day.

Ok so here I am making my debut into the world. Now if you are an astrology enthusiast you understand that astrology does not necessarily tie you to being a certain way, and it doesn't rightfully predict everything about you but I do think there is something to it.

What I think astrology does is explains the energy in your life and your potential challenges and possibilities. Nevertheless, it is said that a Sagittarian born on November 24th; well we seem to do everything by our personality. And boy do I have

personality! Our temperament attracts people to us and our disposition projects an aura of youth and charm. We may seem like lightweights when it comes to dealing with life but we are truly emotionally and spiritually strong. It is said that we are remarkably intelligent yet we don't need to be identified with it to drive our ego. Emotionally and spiritually strong? Geez, if only I knew then what I know now.

I am the Archer, the Centaur. I am Fire! We Sagittarians hold a disposition of cheerfulness and optimism at our core. Innately curious, keeps us more interested in the adventures of tomorrow rather than fixation on the mistakes of the day. I loathe stagnation and believe and delight in change. There is a restlessness within me that I've come to terms with over the years and I disdain the mundane which I'm pretty sure has hurt some of my relationships.

    I am an extremely proud and independent woman and it takes everything in me to ask for help. I'm a warrior, truly a free spirit and straightforward so what you see with me is what you get. I shoot my arrows; always aiming for the distant horizon. Not worrying about the here and now, but staying focused on grabbing the higher light! The light of my creativity.

    I believe my affection for music was solidified at the age of 5 or 6 years old, when I got this thing called a Show N Tell Record Player-Slide Show. It was a little plastic record player with a TV screen where you could view slide movies. The top of the record player played 45 or 33 rpm records. The TV screen played slides from these Picturesound Program books that were records and slides telling various children's stories. While the record was playing, the slide would move up to the next scene. There were many different Picturesound books like History and Science. Of course, my favorites were the fairy tales like Winnie the Pooh, Sesame Street and Disney's Cinderella, Snow White and the Seven Dwarfs. I would sit for hours on end playing the records, watching and singing to the slideshows over and over and over. Music for me was an imaginative and divine experience because it involved expression of feelings. I think children are drawn to music so fiercely because we don't have the capacity or words to express ourselves and need positive ways to release our emotions. Add to that my parents constantly playing music in our house. My folks played our records on this brown fake wood

Magnavox Hi-Fi console. It was a stereo cabinet that took up almost the entire wall of our living room. The top of the cabinet had these sliding panels. Inside the left panel held the AM/FM radio with the dials that were about the size of an Oreo cookie for loudness, bass, treble and radio tuner. Next to it was the record player with metal arm that encased the steel needle and on the other side was the rack that held the 45's.

On Saturday mornings we'd have to get up and clean the house and my mom would throw on some Fleetwood Mac, David Bowie, Linda Ronstadt, Miriam Makeba, and then play some top 40 R&B like Gladys Knight & the Pips, The Temptations, Stevie Wonder, Sly & the Family Stone, Chaka Khan, Aretha, Al Green, Roberta Flack, Jackson 5, The Emotions and for good measure would add in some oldies like Sam Cooke, Otis Redding, Martha & the Vandellas or the Supremes just to change it up. If my mother really loved a song, she had a habit of taking the time sit and write out the lyrics. Every family gathering with aunts, uncles and cousins who lived about 12 brownstones from our apartment building, there were always records playing. Some of my aunts and uncles actually sang with amateur groups in the late 50's and 60's. My grandmother and great aunts always seemed to be humming some tune while cooking up something good and tasty in the kitchen, washing their collard greens or while rolling out the dough to make biscuits or chicken pastry.

All I knew is that music touched me deeply. How did notes and instruments come together so perfectly to create sounds that evoked emotional responses in people?

Music allowed me to live a lot in my head. If there was a song that touched me in a poignant way, I would sit for hours obsessively playing the record again and again listening to the music only. Then individually listening to the lyrics, then playing it back to hear just the lead vocals, or isolating with my ears particular instruments, then listening only to the background oo's and ah's. Then I'd go back to playing the record yet again trying to identify which instruments I was hearing each time I played it; tapping out the percussion or drum rhythms. I used to love to pour over the liner notes on the inside of the albums. Reading who wrote the songs, which instruments were used for each tune and the musicians who played on the album. I'd sit for hours and imagine what they were like in person or how exciting their life must be as a performer.

To my father's dismay, he could never understand how I could learn every song that was played on the radio or absorb lyrics on a record in five minutes but had so much trouble remembering my multiplication tables. It was nothing for me to listen to music or television while doing my homework.

I felt it helped me in some magical way. I guess he couldn't appreciate my talent for multi-tasking. He didn't understand it and didn't hide his frustration.

Let me tell you a little about the man who raised me, the man I call father but who is not my biological dad. When I mention to people that I grew up in a two parent household and that my folks are actually still together, there always seems to be some surprise and a hint of envy. Some have said that I was fortunate because it was such a rarity to come from a two parent household. But we both know that the grass always seems to look greener on the other side of the fence, right?

While my father was present within our house, he was not present emotionally. He was distant and cold company. Add to that he was also an alcoholic. As a kid it wasn't always easy when my dad was home but it was even more stressful when he had been drinking. I'm not sure when his drinking crossed the line from moderate use to problematic drinking. As a kid and into adulthood I often wondered why he drank so much. Was it to cope with difficulties of growing up in the Jim Crow south? To avoid just feeling bad, or being trapped in a life that he didn't want? He would get drunk with his buddies and then start arguments about stupid nonsense with my mom. I had no words for this in my growing-up years, all I know is that it didn't feel good.

My mom was this sweet and beautiful being, very well-liked at work and in the neighborhood and my friends all loved her. They called her the "cool mom" because she was so inclusive of all the kids on the block. If the ice-cream truck stopped by and we were getting ice-cream, she would make sure every kid who was on our stoop got a treat. She was compassionate, sensitive, fun and lovely. But she also struggled with a lot of stuff that came out behind closed doors at home. She'd cry a lot. She'd hole up in her room. I sometimes felt that she put the responsibility on me to comfort her because she used to have this thing where she would make me comb her hair until she fell asleep before I could even think about going outside to play. This hair combing thing would soothe her in into a restful sleep. Oh, how I hated it. I used to think; why is she making me do this? Why did she make it my job to make her feel better?

She and my dad would have these intense verbal altercations and she'd come out of the room with her face tear- stained, and they would not talk to each other for days or sometimes weeks.

As a child, when it came to my dad, I felt as if I could never do anything right. He made me feel that I was different, an outcast, unwanted. I never understood it; maybe because I wasn't really his off-spring. My father would come in and upset mom and the entire household. We all disliked how he would act when he drank. Perhaps I shouldn't say we. My brother who's four years younger than me has never spoken about those days so I won't speak for him.

What I know for sure is that alcoholism is NOT defined by what you drink, when you drink it, or even how much you drink. It's the EFFECTS of your drinking that defines the problem. You don't have to be a homeless vagabond on skid row and drinking out of a brown paper bag to be an alcoholic. I considered my dad to be a high functioning alcoholic. He was able to hold down a job and provide for his family but just because you're a high- functioning alcoholic doesn't mean you're not putting yourself or your family in danger. Because my dad was habitually intoxicated, and had established patterns of heavy drinking, his drinking did in fact put us in dangerous situations, like driving while drunk.

*Sidebar; although the prerequisite of "seat belts are required in all cars" happened in 1968, the seat belt law did not take place until 1984. So, in the seventies wearing a seatbelt was not mandatory.

I was maybe 7 years old and we had gone upstate to Newburgh, NY to visit some family friends of my fathers. One of his drinking buddies lived there with his woman. They drank all afternoon and late into the evening. My mom leaned over to my dad and mentioned that maybe he should stop drinking because it was getting late and we had to get out on the road. Newburgh is about 60 miles from New York City and the thruway ran along mountainous roads, some of which were on sharp bluffs. We left well after 11pm and got on the road to head back to Brooklyn and I have to say that as a 7 year old it was one of the scariest car rides in my life.

My mom kept telling my dad to slow down going around the mountains. He was intoxicated and didn't want to listen. I remember that late night terrifying car ride home as being very intense and my stomach was in knots. My mom later shared with me that she just quietly said a prayer and white knuckled the car door handle all the way home.

Other demonstrations of my father's alcoholism included a drastic change in his demeanor while drinking, such as consistently becoming angry, belligerent or one time I remember even violent with my mother and then there were the black-outs. When I was about 11 or 12, one Friday night after we had dinner my mom kept on me about washing the dishes. I begged to finish watching some sitcom on TV first. My dad came home late that night stinking drunk. He went into the kitchen without turning on the lights, thinking it was the bathroom and proceeded to take a piss in the kitchen sink. My mom yelled at my dad, he cursed her out and she in turn yelled at me for not washing the dishes when she told me to and was angry with me because she had to throw the dishes away. I was hurt and confused as to why I got the blame. Of course my dad had no recollection of the incident but I never forgot. I always felt that I bared the burden of the misplaced stress from my parents' distant, cold, dysfunctional marriage. Maybe it was because I was the oldest or maybe because I was just hypersensitive or both.

On the surface, things appeared calm between my parents, but as a kid I soaked up the tension in the household until my fragile little nervous system hit overload and began manifesting itself in not being able to eat, nail biting and feeling anxious all the time. Oh how I longed for them to divorce if only so that I didn't have to feel those knots in my stomach and they could both perchance find some happiness; to be happy apart from one another.

The very rare times I can truly say I have ever seen my mom happy was when she would become so fed up she would pack us up and leave my dad and we'd go stay with relatives for a while. However, for the most part I've only know my mother as depressed and unhappy which truly breaks my heart. It's no fun as a daughter to watch your mother who used to be your she-ro get treated this way and doesn't feel she's worthy of being happy. What's even crazier is that although my parents are still together, they have consistently chosen to live in denial about the state of their individual lives and fragmented marriage. My father still treats her poorly, and she still stays and takes it. They both don't know how to effectively communicate with each other and are emotionally stuck. Me, always feeling caught in the middle between two people that have never shown love for one another and in fact loathe each other. Their toxicity causes me discomfort and I feel the need to sometimes disconnect from them every so often because it's such a negative environment to be around them. Also, they have passed on their legacy of poor communication tools to us, their children. Not shutting down is probably the one thing that I have to consistently work on.

What's comical to me is when my mother keeps saying she's going to find a husband for me. I think to myself; how can I trust her judgment to find me a partner when she's not a good role model in the marriage department herself. So when she says this to me, I take it with a grain of salt. What I've learned over the years is this; a young teenager growing up looks to her mom as her main example of how to build friendships, how to be a girl, how to navigate in the world as a woman or as a lover.

And what happens if a mother fails to exhibit these virtues in her own marriage?

The daughter goes out into the world ill equipped with no tools and is confused because she's receiving mixed messages her mother sends to her in regards to what positive relationships should be.

I believe that parents often forget that it's their role as guardians to fill each developing stage of a child with encouragement, psychological and emotional support, unconditional love and positive reinforcement otherwise the child finds an empty hole where their heart should be. That child experiences something that he or she cannot explain and seeks to fill that void by looking in all the wrong places with all the wrong people, making the wrong choices. Most children want to please their parents but if the parents are poor communicators or send mixed messages vis-à-vis *"if faced with adversity within a relationship, we don't talk about it with the other person. That it's acceptable to leave issues unresolved to fester!"* and this was and is the case of my folks.

Now as an adult I can understand that this too was my pattern. Why in some of my past relationships I would just shut down. I held a false belief that it was easier and perhaps even safer to say nothing or do nothing. Therefore, not exposing myself to blame or have to actually tell my partner how I really felt, what I wanted or needed from them.

What I know for sure is that the best gift you can give your kids is to create a good strong marriage with a foundation based on respect. If not, over time, the effects will catch up with you. Family dysfunction and alcohol abuse can affect all aspects of your life and the people in it. Poor communication, unhealthy coping mechanisms, long-term substance abuse, and impaired judgment destroys your emotional stability and your ability to shape and sustain satisfying relationships with your family members.

Alcoholism and alcohol abuse have had a devastating impact on my family. I would say that ninety-five percent of the men in my family were and are alcoholics. The alcohol abusers in my family have gone through divorces, had/have problems with domestic violence, sexual assault, struggle with unemployment, and live in poverty or died broke and alone. What I have learned from this is that even if you're able to succeed at work or hold your marriage together, you can't escape the effects that alcoholism has on your personal relationships.

Another one of my father's black-out moments was when my mom was away in North Carolina because my grandfather Hardy was very ill. My dad had been out drinking. He came home and began ranting and raving. He then broke into a lock box my mom kept important papers in. She got it to keep her credit card bills from prying eyes because my dad wanted to control her monetarily and didn't believe in having credit cards. My father's snooping into her personal papers and being on her back about how much money she spent was the reason she got it in the first place. My dad broke into the lock box, found a credit card statement where there were charges of men's items like underwear and socks on it. My dad proceeded to interrogate me on who my mom was buying underwear for. At the time my uncle was in the military and stationed in Germany so my mom would send him care packages every so often but at the time I didn't know this. But me: saying to my father that "I didn't know who she was sending gifts to" did not help. He refused to believe that I didn't know. He badgered and terrorized me to tears and then threatened me not to go downstairs where my aunts and cousins lived or he would kick my ass all the way back upstairs. When he finally passed out, I packed my book bag and ran away from home around midnight. I ended up walking thirty minutes to my older cousin Evelyn's house. She was hip, beautiful, cool, and politically active in the community. She had all the popular albums and smoked her weed. Thank goodness she was home. Although she had company over; they were sitting in her candle lit living room on the floor listening to Rufus & Chaka Khan and Earth Wind & Fire getting high. After I explained to her what had happened with my father, she made a bed for me on her couch and called my mother in North Carolina the next day.

When I didn't show up for church that Sunday, my best friend Lisa called to ask where I was and my dad couldn't tell her because he had no idea. I wonder if he remembers this incident. If he did, he never spoke of it to me. Drinking puts an enormous strain on the people closest to you.

As a young woman my dad and I didn't always have a decent relationship. At best it was indifferent. We didn't have a lot to say to each other for the most part because he was always on my case about something. He treated my mother with such disregard and notwithstanding was once actually physically violent with her. After I left home for good my mom left my dad for about the 50th time. The relationship that I now have with my dad is a lot different from my younger years. A relationship with him is something that I made a conscious choice to develop when I was in my late twenty's after I moved out and went on tour. I decided to work at trying to understand him. I guess it was easier because of the distance between us. I had a lot of time while on the road, starring out the window to put things in perspective and what type of relationship I wanted to have with him. I still constantly try to work on it with him. He has an aloofness about him and I don't think he knows how to show what he really feels. Maybe he just doesn't recognize it when he feels it. Conceivably he didn't have that type of demonstrative love from his own mother and father so consequently he doesn't know how to express his emotions. He's never been a holding-hands type of man. Actually, I can't ever recall him holding my mother's hand, kissing her, offering her words of encouragement, love or any physical contact. In most situations he is uncomfortable and obstinate. To his children he's awkward; he doesn't know how to reach out.

There were no hugs, no kisses, nothing like that growing up. And I think that with his first wife and kids, my three stepbrothers, they didn't have that either. What's more is I'm guessing he didn't have those things while growing up because it just wasn't done in the south in those days perhaps. I can't blame him. I don't blame him. Oh, believe me as I came of age, I did have a lot of resentment for a while. Often wondering why he would have children if he didn't know how to show them love but later I started to understand a little. Now I've come to terms with it. There are a lot of children who grow up without daddies physically or emotionally and I happen to be one of them. At the end of the day you just have to cut your losses and move on right? I have none of the simple memories other children have with their fathers. I can't reminisce about a day as a family, we went to the movies together, or for a picnic, or school event and everyone got along and were happy to be there. All that I learned from him about intimate relationships is the type of man I didn't want to be with; someone who was stoic, cold, distant, controlling and non-communicative. The positive aspects about relationships is what I've learned on my own by way of trial and error but from my parents, nope, no, nothing.

I'll be sad when he's gone because at the end of the day, he has been the only constant father figure in my life and for that I am forever grateful. He always came through for me when I financially needed help. I want to spend as much time as possible with him before he dies. I don't know if he loves me because he's never said it to me. I guess children must learn to accept that sometimes they're not really loved by their parent(s).

Funny, he's older now so he has a tendency to talk about the same things over and over again. I'm not sure if he even remembers that he's telling the same exact stories that happened a long time ago; ancient stories about his friends or his school days in

North Carolina. With love in your heart you have to pretend you are hearing it for the first time and are really attentive. What's interesting is that when I share with him a story or about my day, he never acknowledges anything I say. He doesn't ask questions or seem interested because he just continues to talk over me or about himself or tell his story as if I've never said anything at all. He never asks about my music projects or my personal relationships. Unless I volunteer the information; Zilch!

He never suggests that we do things together like dinner or a movie unless I do it. What's also amusing to me is I don't think he even knows that I'm writing this book. He has never shown any real interest in my life and the things that I'm passionate about. Nevertheless, when I see him I hug him. I ask about his health, his diet, work, events going on in the news. I make it my intention to be present with him. At the end of the day, I would rather maintain the few good memories than the other side, the dark times. But enough about my father.

My mother and I were once very close. She was my all. In my eyes she could do no wrong. She went to bat with my dad all the time for my brother and my well-being.

She tried to always make everything equal and fair. When in a good mood, she was fun to be around. She loved to read. I loved watching old classic movies with her. I always felt she was so strong going through what she did as a young girl. From her is partly where I get my strength. My mom is also generous to a fault. Because my dad was so tight with a dollar she clashed with him constantly in her attempt to make the house look presentable and beautiful. She fought to make sure we had nice clothes, were cultured in theatre, museums and restaurants and that we were able to participate in the things we were passionate about which were sports and the arts.

Oh, and because of her we had some of the most amazing Birthdays, Thanksgivings and Christmases growing up. I loved these special times because all of my extended family would be around. One Christmas my parents bought me an organ that came with a play by numbers song book. This was one of the best gifts I had ever received. My brother got a set of drums that year. When I got my first AM radio as a birthday gift it was another paramount gift that I cherished. That little AM radio was my pathway to the music of the Carpenters, John Denver, James Taylor, Barbara Streisand, Barry Manilow, The BeeGees, Carly Simon, Joni Mitchell, and Carol King. I was hooked. Music was mine. It understood me and I yearned to understand it. It was mine to have and to own. My little music world!

I also had a very vivid imagination. Due to my shyness I also had an imaginary friend named Lele. My mom being the unflappable parent that she was never questioned my imaginary friend phase. As I got older, I was always joining some choir, taking tap lessons or took up learning different instruments.

She was always telling me "if you go and join another thing…" She softly complained because there were always robes, costumes, dance shoes and sheet music to be made or bought but all the same she always let me march to the beat of my own drum. For this I love her and remain forever indebted.

We lived in three different houses in Bed-Stuy, Brooklyn on the same block for about twenty plus years. I was about four where we first lived at the apartment building at 716 Jefferson Avenue. This is where my brother Chris was brought home when he was born. Around age nine we were at a brownstone at 746 Jefferson Avenue where my two aunts and my cousins lived in the first and second floor apartments. Finally, at the age of fourteen we moved right across the street in another brownstone at 767 Jefferson Avenue.

As a young child of about five or six years old, I always carried within me a feeling of being different; I didn't fit in. I felt that I somehow lived at the edge of a looking-glass world where everyday objects came to life, where flowers and animals took on near-human qualities. I was quiet. I was not interested in the same things that other kids were interested in. I wasn't motivated in the same way. I was also a kid who was bullied. Not bullied like the kids are today. I was bullied beginning from kindergarten until around 3rd grade.

The apartment building we lived in at 716 Jefferson Avenue was maintained by a brown skinned man named Mr. Robinson who was the superintendent of the building and lived on the first floor with his wife and son Michael.

Michael was maybe a few years older than me and always picked on me as I entered or left the building to go to the store, go to school or go down the block to visit my cousins. Michael Robinson bullied me as a little girl and eventually grew up to be abusive, dangerous and ultimately a murderer.

Yes, years later, Michael ended up in a wheel chair and doing time in prison at Rikers Island. You see Michael and one of my girlfriends, Judy from around the way began dating in Junior High School. They were madly in love but were always on-again, off-again. Judy became pregnant while still in high school and Michael became more addicted to drugs and increasingly abusive. They broke up and for a while Judy wouldn't let him visit his daughter.

Finally, Judy agreed on visitation with the baby. However, it was contingent upon Michael's mother having to always be present when the baby came for a visit. On this particular day with his daughter, Michael made a choice to smoke some Angel Dust which is the street name for PCP. To me this is the scariest drug on the planet. Although PCP's street name links it to heaven, this drug is most notorious for its association with sinister and extremely gruesome violent crimes. I think the name should be called Devil Dust because of its fiendish components that drive people to do heinous things. It can bring on violent behavior and hallucinations and causes you to disconnect from yourself and reality.

While his mother was in another room, he took the baby up to the roof of the ten- story apartment building. When his mother realized he was gone with the baby, she called Judy and the police. I remember Judy running from her house which was on our same block but closer to the opposite avenue. She went running down the street crazed with trepidation.

The police arrived and she and the officers tried to talk him down. Michael then jumped off of that same building where I once lived with his first-born child; sixteen month old baby girl, Tynesha Nicole Robinson one fall evening in 1984. I still get chills remembering. Everybody on the block was shaken and dumbfounded. My heart broke for my childhood friend Judy. Michael Robinson; from childhood bully to murderer.

Chapter *Four*

Ooh-oo child
Things are gonna get easier
Ooh-oo child
Things'll get brighter-The Five Stairsteps
"Ooh Child"-Stan Vincent, © EMI Music Publishing, Sony/ATV Music Publishing LLC

Now, for many of us, grammar school is supposed to be a fun experience right? This wonderful experience of getting to play with our classmates, going crazy at recess. Enjoying art, music classes and snack time were all a part of a cheerful grade school life, blending into the fabric of growing up. But what about us kids who were bullied in school or on the playground? If you were; different, smart, talented, and shy, wore glasses, braces or didn't look like most of the other students, you were hassled. In a weird way I guess Darwin was right, those who conform do survive. Those who don't, have to fight for their place in the sun.

When I started school at PS 262, I was introverted, sensitive, smaller and also younger than most of my classmates because my mom fudged my birthdate. In order for a kid back then to start Kindergarten, they had to be five years old. Now, I was only four and my birthdate was in late

November. My mom being the smart woman that she was didn't see the point in having me wait and entire year to start school the following September at the age of five going on six. Although I was shy and cautious, I was comfortable making friends if another kid talked to me. I liked sharing and being the teachers' helper.

At school the bullying began at first with the pulling of my long, thick, dark ponytails. It then proceeded to the taking of the snacks my mother prepared for me each day. There were three girls who could be very cruel and vindictive when they banded together. They were always the popular ringleaders who inspired others to join in with the mockery and frenzy. These kids would just take my apple slices or whatever else little goodies I had in my lunch box. Then began the confiscation of my lunch money. Pretty much every day I came home crying to my mother with a story of being picked on, or made fun of, or having something taken from me.

I remember on a rainy afternoon, I think it was first grade. School had just let out and I had my first fight with this girl named Camille. She had long hair, was fair skinned, big boned and way too tall for 1st grade. She was the ringleader for other kids to bully me, but something happened that day. I was determined not to go home crying. I had had enough of her picking on me and egging on others to do the same. When she approached me as I was crossing the doorway to the outside of the building, she shoved me so hard that I almost fell faced down. Steadying myself, I then spun around on my red Buster Brown

Mary Jane heels and took my little clear plastic umbrella with the yellow ducks on them, closed my eyes real tight and began to swing at her until some teachers grabbed me to make me stop. I then turned to the others who would follow her lead and pointed my umbrella at them daring them. From that day forward Camille and her little cronies never bothered me again, however, with each new school year came with it a new bully that I had to eventually stand up to.

Perhaps this is why I have always had an affinity for the underdog in most situations and now have zero tolerance for any bullshit from adults who bully others. And yes people, I still see grown adults who are on the periphery of my life still trying to bully other adults; be it people in church, at work, at the grocery store, on the subway, former school acquaintances or on social media. I'm sure you know some grown ass people who fit this description don't you?

Anyone who is truthful about their childhood might remember instances of bullying in one of two ways. They were either the victims of the violence themselves or they had been unwilling witnesses to or participants in a bullying incident. The fact is, bullying has been an unfortunate circumstance of life for too many generations of children. Some adults make it sound as if bullying is some new byproduct of the 21st century. It isn't. Bullying has been around as long as the human race. I can't help but think about all the cruel things kids do to each other nowadays with emails, social media, cell phones and texting. It's actually a lot worse today but it's also indicative of the violent times that we live in. Bully's today usually work in groups, picking on other children unable or too afraid to defend themselves; actions that are causing kids to commit suicide. Bullying today is much more ferocious!

I'd like to see bullying be treated like the crime that it is. I'd like to see bullies today under the age of eighteen punished by the same laws as adults. Any physical violence, any threats should be dealt with expeditiously and stiffly. They should be made to understand that society cannot and will not tolerate their actions. No child should have to fear going to school, riding the school bus or going away to camp. The law should not coddle these bullies under the guise that they are still children themselves. Their actions are cruel in manner, deliberately inflicting physical and emotional pain. They need to be made aware of the seriousness of their behavior. Bullies are, at heart, cowards, who only torment those whom they feel cannot fight back. Let these cowards tangle with law enforcement and judges. Make them as scared as they've made their victims.

Let there be no more childhood scars, visible or emotional from the intimidation or domination toward someone who is perceived as being weaker or different.

Despite what people say, I don't always hold the belief that being bullied makes you a better person or builds character; at least not for some kids. For a lot of people, it destroys their identity, sense of self and in some cases their life.

By the time I got to fourth grade I learned to navigate my way around the not so nice kids, traverse my path with the really smart kids, and found solace in being swathed in the circle of creative kids. As I participated in school and outside activities, I became more outgoing, was considered funny, creative, easygoing, bright and the best part was that the bullying had finally stopped and that's when my calling for self-expression became stronger.

The first time I got a taste of being on stage acting was when for Black History Month, I played Harriet Tubman in my first school play at the George E. Wibecam School, PS 309 on Monroe Street in Brooklyn. My parents didn't come that evening to my performance. My mother was too drained to come that night and my dad was somewhere off drinking with his friends. This was pretty much how it would be in the years to follow. Although she came out to support me in some of my performances more than my father, most of the time they were no-shows because of mom being too tired or depressed about something and my dad was just never around or showed interest in being supportive.

Although the school was about six blocks away from my house on Jefferson Avenue for some reason my mother let me go by myself. Was she not concerned with my safety? I remember being a bit apprehensive not about my performance but because it was winter and it got dark outside early. I had never walked to my school at night so I ended up running the entire way there. To this day I can't believe she just let me go by myself. But then again it was the 70's.

The scene was playing Harriet Tubman who was running away from her slave master. She got caught and was beaten. I remember writhing on the stage and screaming out in pain as the imaginary whip hit me. There in that big auditorium I heard a few kids giggling which then morphed into laughter as I continued to act out this whipping scene. Then the entire hall exploded with cackling.

I was a bit heart broken and confused about them laughing about a slave being beaten. But then again, that's when the acting bug really hit me and I knew I wanted to be on stage. I didn't care that they laughed at least I got a reaction. I was a dreamer who dreamt of greatness on the stage whether it be singing or acting. I didn't know how I would get there all I knew was that I just had to do it.

Over the years I continued to sing. I learned every song on the radio, made up stories and acted them out in my room, joined my junior choir in church, took trumpet, xylophone and piano lessons. I took tap and ballet lessons and in between my mom took my brother and me into the city to see shows and my aunt, uncle, cousins I would sing and dance when we were all together. This is how my love of the arts was birthed and nurtured.

Growing up I would often hear adults on my block say within ear shot of me, how I was such an idealist and lived with my head in the clouds way too much. My teachers even wrote in my report cards about how much I daydreamed in class. This much was true. I've never seemed to lose my sense of wonder and love of the arts. I believe that being allowed to tap into my creative spirit helped me develop a strong sense of self.

And then there was my favorite teacher Mrs. Ruby Ramos who wore this badass afro. It was big enough that it sat like a halo around her head. She wore colorful dashiki's and when she walked into a room everyone paid attention. She lived two blocks away from us. Her children Victor and Lisa were also in the same public schools in our community. She took me under her wing because I was such a voracious reader. Another gift I got from my mom.

I remember her telling me to always be a credit to my race and that I could be anything that I wanted to be. Be a credit to my race? Huh? What? That was way too deep for me to really comprehend. For goodness sake, I was only eight or nine years old. I can't say that I truly knew what she meant, what that phrase meant at the time but as I got older and to this day I remember her words of wisdom and cherish them. Because of her and my mother, I did become aware of how I presented myself to the world when I was out in public; my walk, how I spoke, my manners. She fostered my love of reading, art and music. Mrs. Ramos also made me believe that if I wanted to be a singer or actor, if I wanted to do anything in the arts that it was possible. I could express myself anyway I wanted. I just needed to always conduct myself with self-respect and confidence and go for it. All that I desired was inside of me. All I had to do was trust my inner voice.

Now, how's that for the influence of a public school education and the inspiration and power of a third grade teacher! She is with me always.

Music helped me sharpen my intuitiveness, to feel comfortable in my introspection, value optimism and remain forever hopeful no matter the situation. People throughout my life that have crossed paths with me, some have said that I saw life through rose-colored glasses. Couldn't help it though! I've always been a positive, hopeful person. I've always held the belief that things will always work out. I wonder what Ms. Ramos would say about Barack Obama becoming the first African American President of the United States. He is definitely a credit to his race wouldn't you say? Ms. Ruby Ramos lost her battle with cancer and died during the late 70's from the malignance. I hope that she is proud of me. One of my favorite quotes that reminds me of her is:

"Music is the purest form of art; therefore true poets seek to express the universe in terms of music. The singer has everything within him. The notes come out from his very life. They are not materials gathered from outside." - *Rabindranath Tagore*

Chapter *Five*

When the moon is in the seventh house
And Jupiter aligns with Mars
and peace will guide the planets
and love will steer the stars.
This is the dawning of the Age of Aquarius,
Age of Aquarius…- Fifth Dimension
Aquarius/Let The Sunshine In-Musical Hair-James Rado ,Gerome Ragni
Galt, MacDermot

Okay, so if you've gotten this far in my story perchance you've figured out by now that I am not a Christian and therefore do not believe in GOD. There. I've said it! I am a Buddhist. Buddhism is a nontheistic religion, i.e., it does not believe in a supreme creator being a.k.a. God. I just don't believe in something or someone that exists outside of me. Perhaps this is what eventually attracted me to Buddhism. Now, I've always been curious about religion. In fact, I find most religions fascinating. Most of my extended family were Southern Baptists.

My mother and father were not religious people and the beautiful thing about my mom was she didn't "make" us go to church. She let us discover and decide on religion for ourselves.

I was baptized in the church next door to the Brooklyn brownstone we lived in at Universal Baptist

No Ordinary Love

Church by Reverend Pope. Reverend Pope was this short, pudgy, dark skinned man who was loved by all. While he was a well respected man in the community, he would also get a little fresh with us young girls. He would hug us just a little bit too long, and tell jokes that were filled with sexual innuendo. As I grew up, I became more involved in church activities. I was always in the choir. I joined the Junior Usher Board and later began to attend Bible Studies every Wednesday night, and even visited prisons during the holidays to help spread the word through song.

At some point, I began to question church leaders, elders and teachers on bible passages, sermons and how they treated members of the church and in the community who were different. They were very hypercritical of other folks. It seemed they could never really give me concrete answers that would satisfy my longing to know the why's. They became exasperated with me and my questioning the things that just didn't make sense to me. I slowly stopped attending meetings. I stopped traveling with them to prisons. I dropped out of the Junior Usher Board and choir and stopped attending church all together. I began to study Catholicism but it felt more rigid than my Baptist upbringing.

For a brief moment I was going to Jehovah Witness meetings with a high school friend at the time until it began feeling like no one there was ever happy and their doctrine didn't make sense to me either. They didn't celebrate anything about life. They were just as judgmental and oppressive and Christians. It was my experience that critical thinking was looked upon as negative.

I even had an argument with a Witness who told me that children do in fact pay for the sins of their parents. My question to her was, so if my mother was a prostitute that means I'm also going to hell? My questions were never really answered, just a lot of bible quotes. Suffice it to say, that was the last time I attended a meeting. What's amusing is, decades later my mom decided to become a Jehovah Witness which became and is a source of contention for me. But to each his own, right? Everything is not for everybody.

I was about twelve or thirteen years old and I wasn't feeling well. On this particular day my mom brought home this book called the Bhagavad-Gita on Hinduism. Not sure where she got it. I think someone gave it to her and because it had these beautiful colored pictures of Hindi Gods she didn't want to throw it away so she passed it off to me. Although reading Bhagavad-Gita spiritually felt a bit better it still wasn't right for me. I was even approached by Scientologists in Times Square one summer evening after an audition and given some material to read along with a book by L. Ron Hubbard. As I started reading it, I thought this is definitely NOT for me.

And then there was Buddhism. I didn't become a Buddhist right away but just the bits and pieces that I began learning spoke to me in a way that I hadn't felt about any other religion or philosophy that I had read about or pursued. It was a practice that celebrated life, humanity, nature, love and compassion. You held accountability for your own life, responsibility of the energy and light you bring into the world and how to align heart and soul with the rhythm of the universe. There was no blame, no jealous or ruthless god. No judgments, everyone was welcome.

In my quest, I found Buddhism had nothing to do with "salvation" in the future. It teaches you how to live in the present moment, to see your life clearly. There is no guilt, no shame or oppressive rules and no angry, vengeful Deities. Buddhism's lone goal is to attain enlightenment in the here and now if you are willing to do the work of your own human revolution. People often ask me about my beliefs in contrast to when I was a Christian versus becoming a Buddhist. Here are some corresponding concepts in Christianity and Buddhism that I laid side by side before I made my decision to practice Buddhism.

• The Divine:	God	Life
• The Origin:	Uncreated, Unborn	Uncreated, Unborn
• Time Span:	God is eternal	Life is Eternal
• The Material & Spiritual:	Separate	Inseparable
• Good and Evil:	Separate	Inseparable
• The Afterlife:	Two external places	Rebirth
• Heaven and Hell:	Two external places	Two internal states

In comparison, in Christianity, "God" is "somewhere out there" while Buddhahood exists within me. When Christian's pray they are requesting redemption from an all-knowing, almighty and omnipresent father figure. We believe in the Mystic Law of Cause and Effect which is the spiritual unseen link between the stirring inner reality of my life and how it/I relate to the rest of the outside world. As

Buddhists we chant and it can be used as a method of meditation. The basic practice of Nichiren Buddhism consists of chanting the phrase Nam-myoho-renge-kyo to your own personal Gohonzon. In addition, there is the twice daily practice of gongyo, which involves the recitation of two key chapters of the Lotus Sutra, followed with more chanting of the above mentioned phrase.

We chant to develop a higher and more expansive life- condition. We chant about making the right decisions and taking the right actions. We chant with the dominant intention to be happy and for the happiness of others.

When I practiced Christianity, I was taught that man was fundamentally flawed and needed forgiving, whereas Buddhism promises that we are all in essence brilliant and just need to continue to polish our lives in order for that brilliance to always shine through. I then began to learn about the Four Noble Truths and the Eight Fold Paths.

The Four Noble Truths encompasses;

The Truth of Suffering; The Buddha declared that this world is full of suffering; that actual existence including birth, decrepitude, sickness and death is suffering and sorrow. This is called the Truth of Suffering.

The Truth of the Cause of Suffering; The cause of human suffering lies in ignorance and Karma. Ignorance and its resulting Karma have often times been called "desire" or craving.

The Truth of the Cessation of Suffering; The extinguishing of all human ignorance and Karma results in a state known as Nirvana.

The Truth of the Path to the Cessation of Suffering;

The Truth of the Path to the Cessation of Suffering is the Noble Eight-fold Path.

In a nutshell, the first two **Noble Truths** is the diagnoses, the problem (suffering) and identified its cause. The third **Noble Truth** is the realization that there is a cure. The fourth **Noble Truth**, in which the **Buddha** set out the **Eightfold Path**, is the prescription or the way to achieve and release all living beings from suffering.

The Eight-Fold Path being the fourth of the Four Noble Truths is the first of the Buddha's teachings. All the teachings flow from this foundation.

1. **Right Views** - to keep ourselves free from prejudice, superstition and delusion and to see the true nature of life.
2. **Right Thoughts** - to turn away from the evils of this world and to direct our minds towards honesty and virtue.
3. **Right Speech** - to refrain from pointless and harmful talk to speak kindly and courteously to all.
4. **Right Conduct** - to see that our deeds are peaceful, benevolent, compassionate and pure; to live the Teaching of the Buddha daily.

5. **Right Livelihood** - to earn our living in such a way as to entail no evil consequences.

6. **Right Effort** - to direct our efforts continually to the overcoming of ignorance and selfish desires.

7. **Right Mindfulness** - to cherish good and pure thoughts for all that we say and do arise from our thoughts.

8. **Right Meditation** - to concentrate our will on the Buddha and how he lived his life and his teachings.

Subsequently these eight paths can be put into the categories of precepts, meditation and wisdom and is the route to practicing Buddhism via the Three Vehicles of Learning. By following theses precepts we learn to master our body and mind. Through mediation we learn to unify our mind. Wisdom is accomplished by the practice of the above two and through this wisdom all ignorance and passions are cut off and thereby the true state of Enlightenment is then realized.

Overall, I liked that there were no concepts of sin, of guiltiness, or what felt like a stifling obedience to an external power.

Buddhists don't believe in a god because they believe in life and humanity. They believe that each human being is precious and important, that all have the potential to develop into a Buddha or enlightened human being. They believe that humans can outgrow ignorance and irrationality and see things as they really are. They believe that hatred, anger, spite and jealousy; your fundamental darkness can be replaced by love, patience, generosity and kindness. That all of this is within the grasp of each person if they make the effort. The effort is your own individual human revolution.

Buddhists are not troubled with rewards in the hereafter. There is no heaven or hell as a place to travel to. Heaven and hell only exist within each one of us. We are not concerned about starting wars because others don't agree with our philosophy. Instead we deal with the never ending circle of birth and death. In this world and in all worlds, there are many beginnings and ends. Life from the point of view of Buddhism has no starting place. It just keeps going and going. These were just some of the reasons why I was attracted to Buddhism. Now, I don't hold the belief that Buddhism is superior to other "organized" religions. I think this flawed premise is part of what's wrong with the world today with religious fanatics, terrorist and hate groups. As a matter of fact, Buddhism has some serious flaws as well. Many people are attracted to a very shallow version of it, a Buddhism only of the mind and not really fixed in reality. For example, traditional Buddhism is concerned with subduing the ego, which is the very opposite of the contemporary American disposition. For me Buddhism spoke to my heart, my uniqueness and self- expression.

As a Buddhist I respect and don't have a problem with people who believe in nothing. I certainly don't have a problem with others who do hold a concept of god, if they use this concept for the peace, happiness and the welfare of mankind. But I have zero tolerance with those who abuse this God perception by bullying people in order to introduce this belief for their own benefit and by way of using ulterior motives. I think all people should be allowed to work and seek their own redemption without any undue interfering from other causes. Yes, people should uphold their beliefs and concepts, however it should be done without fanaticism or malice or vindictiveness. I don't contest others in regard to their religious influences, and I expect reciprocal treatment in regard to my own beliefs and practices.

What I know for sure is that my Buddhist practice keeps my life in rhythm with the Universe. The way that I breathe, the way that my heart beats. Just like way the waves smash the beach, the way tides are affected by the moon, the way planets rotate round and round and round the sun, the way the moon orbits around planets. The rhythm of life, this is it in a nutshell! That's what I strive for.

This universal cadence in this dimension to me, simply put, is "alignment and balance". Yep, that's it! That's all there is.

To me the pulse of the Universe is essentially like two colossal massive scales and sometimes they tip a little bit to the left and sometimes they tip a little bit to the right. However, they always find a way to come back to the center, always! Often times it takes a bit longer than we would like but it always comes back to the middle. That's the way the cosmos work. This is the law that controls everything in the

Universe. Things go one way and then they come back another; there's a definite rhythm in this Universe of ours. What goes out comes in, what goes around comes around. Whatever you send forth into the universe it boomerangs back; hence, the beautiful words "…on earth as it is in heaven…" Some of us forget that. Sure, I forget that from time to time but I've been fortunate to have and had numerous spiritual teachers guiding me along the way.

Just to name a few; my charming, warm, grounded, focused, childhood sister-friend, Lisa M. Gray. The beautiful, effervescent, smart, talented, witty, Dr. Michele Sweeting-DeCaro my high school sister-friend. Some of my other more well-known spiritual teachers have been Louise Hay, Patricia Moreno, Daisaku Ikeda, Wayne Dyer, Oprah Winfrey, Esther-Abraham and Jerry Hicks, Marianne Williamson, Immaculee Illibagiza, Ishmael Beah, Joseph Campbell, Marianne Pearl, Maya Angelou and Tina Turner, Elizabeth Gilbert and Iyanla Vanzant.

Now I have not met them all face to face but they have taught me valuable lessons with their astuteness, life experiences, struggles and triumphs. I came across these teachers whose philosophies have echoed what I felt within physically and emotionally and who have helped me along the way to become more self-aware, more of who I am meant to be. And for this I offer my deepest appreciation and sincere gratitude.

In Buddhism we call this consciousness or enlightenment and the connection of all things. These sages have offered me great wisdom through their quotes, books, audios, classes, workshops and films. I think in sharing their struggles and practices, their goal is not only to transmit knowledge or understanding as much as it is to somehow bring about an appreciation within each individual, within me, the student's own pre-existent nature. Consequently, as a result my consciousness or mindfulness was awakened.

This is a much more subtle thing than simply teaching someone a skill or understanding. It is not that a spiritual teacher never provides spiritual knowledge or understanding, but imparting to me the student that this knowledge or understanding by itself cannot be the actual objective. You've heard the quote it's not about the destination it's about the journey?

As divine students we can have a wide-ranging knowledge of spiritual principles, and yet still not truly accepted those principles as being inherent within our own lives.

What I know for sure is that spiritual teachers or mentors may teach a lot or they may not teach anything at all but it depends on what we, me the student needs in that exact moment to experience the deeper recognition of my real true nature, my higher self. The essence of who I am at my core has been drawn to this collection of "physical and nonphysical teachers" who have come together as sort of a rendezvous to help me in understanding myself in context to the universe and its most powerful force: the rules of the Mystic Law or some of you may call it the Law of Attraction. Some of the rules of the universe I have learned are about co-existence and the interrelatedness of all things, taking responsibility for my life and relationships and honoring differences and otherness. Did you know that the soul has its way of focusing on true self-expression and self-actualization?

Pierre Teilhard de Chardin (May 1st 1881 – April 10th 1955) who was a French Jesuit priest and mystic philosopher who worked to understand evolution and faith, once said "We are not human beings having a spiritual experience; we are spiritual beings having a human experience." Ahh, let's sit with that for a moment. Yes, in our physical form our souls or higher-self are always seeking experiences which offer personal fulfilment within life on the physical plane.

These spiritual instructors have given me hope, insight, the tools and ability to challenge my life from a different angle; from within. The premise of the work for me is this: we are all connected. Everything we do affects other people. Every thought, every word we utter, every emotion we feel emits a vibrational charge in our lives and the environment around us.

When we make a practice of choosing negative thoughts or emotions, we flood our physical, mental and emotional bodies with a lower vibrational energy and we continue to get more of the same negativity in our lives. Abraham Hicks in one of his workshops said, " when we continue to beat the drum of what we don't want, what we don't like, what's not working, complaining about lack or not having enough, whining about why others have more than us, the universe will just give you more negativity." Hence, the Universal Law of Attraction.

No one can continue to operate in a vacuum of negative energy without it taking its toll in all areas of our lives. These lower energies actually drain our human energy tanks and if we continue to do this day in and day out sooner or later the physical, mental and emotional body breaks down, which then creates disease. The pre-fix for disease is Latin, meaning "apart from." Disease is just you being apart from or disconnected from the essence of who you really are at your core which is a vibrational energy that is natural, simplistic, effortless, ease.

Louise Hay mentions in her book Heal Your Life, that "there are really just two mental patterns that contribute to disease: Fear and Anger. Anger can show up as impatience, irritation, frustration, criticism, resentment, jealousy or bitterness.

She states that these are all thoughts that poison the body and when we let go of this burden, all the organs in our body begin to function properly."

Likewise, when we decide to feed ourselves with the experience of positive emotions, we fill up our physical, mental and emotional tanks. When the tanks are full we are running in top form. We then in turn start experiencing optimum health and wellbeing. We become more focused, grounded, creative, happy and loving.

As time passed and I came of age little did I know that this philosophy would serve me well on my life voyage. This knowledge that I was acquiring was for my most important spiritual journey that lay ahead of me.

You see, I've learned that the universe is always causing us to expand our lives whether we want or are ready to expand or not. The universe is always giving us challenges or obstacles for our growth and development. Each trial brings us closer to who we were meant to be, closer to our higher self, and closer to the Divine within. When we resist against this expansion, THIS is when we feel the discord, the conflict within us.

As Esther/Abraham put it so eloquently, "When you're feeling frustrated, overwhelmed, angry, worried and fearful, all it means is that you are not keeping up with you. You are not in alignment with the genius source creator which is you. The universe created contrast for your life to expand and when you resist, you refuse to go. When you refuse to go, you are out of alignment with your higher self, who you really are."

Think about it, our lives can only expand by way of the contrast in our environment. Some may call this conflict, challenges, or obstacles. Using the word contrast just feels/sounds better to me. Great things happen to us, good things happen and so do bad things but no matter what, contrast has its way of sharpening your focus. What you focus on you get more of. So if you have a complaining, negative vibration then you are consistently creating more of it in your life. Having contrast in our lives helps us to define what it is that we really want while on this planet. It assists us with knowing what we want and what we don't want. As my spiritual guide Esther/Abraham has shared, "Contrast exists as kind of a variety...There are things that you see as unwanted contrast that others see as wanted. Without the contrast there would be no improvement to knowing what it is that you really desire.

Ok, warning, I'm going to use my candy analogy. Oh, I forgot to mention that I'm a bit of a candy fiend.

Now as I see it everything always comes down to this; perception and free will.

Let's say you go into Dylan's Candy Store over on Third Avenue and E. 60th. You get to scope the huge variety of candy right? Now, you might not want the Strawberry Twizzler's but you wouldn't just demand that they be taken away from the counter. You just don't pick that one. Pick what you want, the Swedish Fish and Jolly Ranchers and leave the rest. That's the way contrast or challenges in your life work. It is there for you to choose from. I tell you this, the contrast in my life teaches me to be clear about what it is that I really desire for my life. Therefore, I'm incessantly making modifications of the requests that I propel out into the universe. So instead of me stating what I don't like about this or that, I revise my statements into "wouldn't it be wonderful if" or "what I actually like about this or that is..." Contrast goes hand in hand with my desires. It is the distinction that creates my desires. By knowing what I DON'T want, it actually causes me to know what I DO want. When your life is expanding due to the dissimilarity in your life you are really expanding into your higher self, the person you were meant to be.

This I know to be true, is that when I am in vibrational alignment with who I really am, then the universe without fail lines me up with people and circumstances who are ready to engage with me. See, the universe will always let you know you're in alignment by way of signs, feeling good, positive situations and meeting the right people. People who you're supposed to come into contact with for a short stint or a life time. People who needed to engage with you because there was a message to be given, something you or they needed to learn, have asked and in the asking are ready to hear, and on it goes.

I must admit that sometimes, I do feel vibrationally exhausted especially with all of the anarchy going on in the world but I think it's important for people to ask themselves, do they see their world as a bad place or as a good place? How we see the world, will determine how the world reacts to you. Esther/Abraham says, "This contrasting experience acts as the catalytic experience we all knew it would be when we decided to come here." I love that quote!

Chapter *Six*

A Love Supreme, A Love Supreme
A Love Supreme, A Love Supreme-John Coltrane
A Love Supreme-John Coltrane-Jowcol Music [BMI], © 1964 MCA Records,
Inc

Ok, I didn't mean to get all woo, woo, woo on you. It's easy for me to get into a discussion about consciousness, awareness and oneness with the cosmos. All these topics I know, can honestly feel sometimes kind of hefty to talk about. A bit too serious almost. But I have to say that what I'm coming to find is the more I open my arms and surrender, each time I let go of thoughts and beliefs that no longer serve me and I reach for thoughts that feel better, carry out self-inquiry or allow things to be as they are, I have an understanding that they are all fundamental ways to release my ego's resistance to what is. This then becomes the foundation for my divine self that longs to be a part of the human experience. I see that the more I expand both my consciousness of All That Is (the light and the dark of me) as well as accepting that everlasting bliss is always present in my life, then the more I continue to live a purposeful life as an expression of and celebration of joy and love. Honestly, these days I find myself trying not to get so caught up about "enlightenment or nirvana" as it relates to my Buddhist practice any longer but instead enjoy living this life experience in this moment, here and now, fully as I AM. What I'm discovering on this trip is that, as so many spiritual leaders have said, it is *"YOU."*

YOU are the point, *YOU* are the Divine, and the Divine is within *YOU*. *YOU* are the gift. *YOU* are what you have been looking for. The *'I AM'* is it! Just to *BE* what you ARE is already a tremendous blessing, and to be in living expression of this blessing by having this life experience allows us to both know and *EXPERIENCE* who we really are. This is what grounds the spiritual energy into the physical, uniting the up there with down here piece, and bringing paradise down to earth as is often said. And so the point is just to enjoy the love that is you, the joy that is you, the well-being that is you, here and now.

Esther/Abraham Hicks articulates that "feeling good indicates you're in alignment with your divine guidance system and headed in the direction of your highest good." So when we are feeling short-tempered, unfulfilled, annoyed, jealous, bitter, resentful, or any other emotion that doesn't feel "good" it just means your Higher Self is giving you guidance, signposts that you have veered off of your path. When we are off the path all it means is that we are hiding our divine self from our human self.

I want my journey here in this body to be an expedition of me learning about myself, my higher self and what type of darkness and light I bring into the world, merging my spirituality and my humanness. I'm not sure if this was a conscious choice at first but as a traveler on this journey so far, at some point I did feel that I had become awake. Conscious.

I know we all talk about being chill and going with the flow. Yet, there are times I allow the outside world to stall my flow and some days I don't feel very chill but my goal is to get to the place of consistently being able to flow from a place of oneness with the Universe and there is only the flow of life. There are no separate parts, just this one harmonious flow of many apparent individuals. To paraphrase the Sufi poet Rumi,

"You are the entire ocean, and the entire ocean is contained in each drop, expressing itself as each drop. We can allow everything to be as it is and find that there's this natural intuitive movement within us to flow this way or that, as if we have an inner sense of what the next step is and how to respond spontaneously in any moment. No rules. Just natural flow. Simple. Light. Ease."

Living It!

Chapter *Seven*

Ain't nothin' gonna to break my stride
Nobody's gonna slow me down, oh-no
I got to keep on movin'
Ain't nothin' gonna break my stride
I'm running and I won't touch ground
Oh-no, I got to keep on movin'-Matthew Wilder
"Break My Stride" by Matthew Wilder, Greg Prestopino

Just like a truly Greek tragedy, our destiny becomes obvious to everyone from the first moment, of the first scene on stage. That our real lives, just like a play can be profound like a script lying there on a shelf for anyone perceptive enough to read it. I feel that I still have work to do in this lifetime left over from the one before. And just like those heroes, she-ros and antagonists in Greek literature, those whom the gods took kindly to, they also gave a lot of pain. When much is given, much is expected right?

The pain these characters faced was considered worthy because it was the catalyst that moved them along faster to that place where they were meant to be; to their destiny.

I only know that each one of us is dealt a hand that most of us seem to play and sometimes a few of us proclaim and shout to the heavens that "we don't want these cards that we are given", or we don't want to play anymore or would like to make a request of the dealer to "please deal again."

Many events in my life have been comically tragic or just a tragic comedy I suppose. The stories that tragedies always deal with stems from larger-than-life melodic poetry. The heart of all tragic plots were most often folklores treated in the oral traditions of old-fashioned epics.

With that said, welcome to the epic of my life.

Chapter *Eight*

The phone rings in the middle of the night
My father yells what you gonna do with your life
Oh daddy dear you know you're still number one
But girls they want to have fun
Oh girls just want to have fun...- Cyndi Lauper
"Girls Just Wanna Have Fun"-Sony/ATV Tunes LLC, Warner/Tamerlane
Publishing, Rellla Music Corp.

So, here I am! It's the morning of June 21st 1984. I got myself ready. I wore a grey silk drop-waist dress `a la circa 1920's from Saks Fifth Avenue. It had a white laced collar with big pleats at the bottom and a gray sash. I coifed my hair in a kind of 1940's up do, a little pressed powder, eyeliner, mascara and red lipstick. There! I was really ready. Ready to begin the next phase of my life. I was about to graduate from High School. Now mind you this special day should've taken place June of 1983 but, well you know how it is right? That feeling of freedom from the watchful eyes your parents; let's just say I wasn't as focused as I needed to be during my first time around.

I quickly learned my lesson for my re-occurring role as a high school senior. With that said, I had spent the last four years of my life which should have been three years, with some really amazing, incredible, cool, talented people. Although we came from different socio-economic backgrounds all over New York, we had one thing in common and this was our love and passion for the arts. We were creative minds longing to express ourselves as singers, musicians, painters and sculptors.

I was graduating from the famed High School of Music & Art and just in case you've been living on another planet or under a rock but came out long enough to catch a little movie called Fame, the one with Irene Cara, yes well that was my school. This was one of the most prestigious specialized high schools in New York City at the time.

You probably know the school now as LaGuardia High School of Performing Arts. You see back then there were two separate divisions under the same Fiorello LaGuardia umbrella. There was Music & Art or (M&A) as we call it and Performing Arts (PA) as THEY called themselves. We were a bit competitive don't you know, but at the end of the day there is definitely love for everyone weather you were M&A or PA. One school was for musicians, singers and artists and PA was for actors, dancers, musicians and playwrights. Here are some notable alumni of both schools:

Actors: Jennifer Aniston, Ellen Barkin, Richard Benjamin, Julie Bovasso*, Adrien Brody, Charles Busch, Thom Christopher, Victor Cook, Keith David, Michael DeLorenzo, Dom DeLuise*, Thom Christopher, Dagmara Dominczyk, Omar Epps, Sarah Michelle Gellar, Cliff Gorman*, Jackee Harry, Anna Maria Horsford, Paula Kelly, Hal Linden, Priscilla

Lopez, Sonia Manzano, Janet Margolin*(Annie Hall, Ghost Busters, Murder She Wrote), James Moody(Fame, D.C. Cab, Bad Boys, New York Undercover, Law & Order, The Best Man, The Last Dragon) Keith Nobbs (New York Undercover, The Sopranos, Law & Order, and Law & Order: Criminal Intent) Al Pacino (The Godfather, Scarface, Dog Day Afternoon, Any Given Sunday, Angels in America, Serpico) Sarah Paulson (Studio 60 on the Sunset Strip, Game Change, Martha Marcy May Marlene, and American Horror Story.) Elizabeth Peña (Rush Hour, Free Willy Boston Public, Without a Trace, CSI-Miami) Brock Peters*(Porgy & Bess, To Kill A Mockingbird, Star Trek-Deep Space Nine), Suzanne Pleshette*(Alfred Hitchcock- The Birds, Bob Newhart), Tony Roberts(Woody Allen's-Annie Hall, Radio Days, Stardust Memories, Hannah and Her Sisters, A Midsummer Night's Sex Comedy, The Taking of Pelham One Two Three. Serpico, Amityville 3-D) Jennifer Salt, Helen Slater as Ruthless People, The Secret of My Success, and City Slickers, Smallville, The Lying Game.) Wesley Snipes (Michael Jackson's Bad video, Mo Better Blues, Jungle Fever, New Jack City, White Men Can't Jump,) Susan Strasberg* (The Virginian, The Invaders, Bonanza, The Streets of San Francisco, Night Gallery, McCloud, The Big Valley, Remington Steele, The Rockford Files). Glynn Turman (Cooley High, Hero Aint Nothin But a Sandwich, Five On the Black Hand Side, A Different World, Buffalo Solider, The Wire) Jessica Walter (Play Misty for Me, Columbo, Arrested Development) Marlon Wayans (I'm Gonna Git You Sucka, The Wayans Bros., Scary

Movie, Scary Movie 2, White Chicks, Little Man, Dance Flick, Requiem for a Dream, G.I. Joe: The Rise of Cobra) Billy Dee Williams(Mahogany, Lady Sings the Blues, Star Wars Episode V: The Empire Strikes Back, Star Wars Episode VI: Return of the Jedi. Northern Calloway* (David- Sesame Street, A Mid-Summers Night Dream, Pippin), Jackee Harry (227, Sister Sister, Women of Brewster Place, Amen).

Entertainers/Musicians/Singers, HipHop Artists, Lyricists, Songwriters: Dana Dane, Lisa Fischer, Ben Harney, Janice Ian, Nikki Minaj, Alicia Keys,: Eartha Kitt*, Shari Lewis*, Melissa Manchester, Liza Minnelli, Peter Nero, Laura Nyro*, Felix Pappalardi, Freddie Prinze*, Slick Rick, Paul Stanley, Suzanne Vega, Ben Vereen, Eric Weissberg, Peter Yarrow, Carole Bayer Sager, Marilyn Bergman.

The New York City Mayor, Fiorello H. LaGuardia started the high school in 1936, and described it as the proudest achievement of his administration. The school was made up of three departments: Art, Instrumental Music, and Vocal Music. We, Music & Art alumni lovingly refer to the building as "The Castle," which is a reference to the design of its gothic towers, and the decorative gargoyles done in an eccentric and playful style that the Landmarks Commission defines as "finials in the shape of creatures bearing shields."

For us lords and ladies of the castle, there were tower rooms with these remarkable theatrical acoustics, which we used as choral practice rooms. There was a large gymnasium that highlighted the large Tudor-arch-shaped windows on two sides and at certain times during the day they streamed the warm sunlight into the gym. The auditorium also had excellent acoustics, and featured these diamond-shaped amber windows that during daylight hours would cast a warm glow on its dark wood interior. The iron ends of the auditorium seats had a casting with an image of the Tudor window arches in the gymnasium.

In 1984, at summers end, Music & Art and our sister school Performing Arts, were merged into a new school which became the Fiorello H. LaGuardia High School of Performing Arts at a new building in the Lincoln Center area of Manhattan where the movie West Side Story was filmed. Using shorthand, we now just called it LaGuardia. We were the last graduating class from the "Castle on the Hill." The castle is still there, located in the Hamilton Heights neighborhood of Harlem near the campus of the City College of New York and St. Nicholas Park.

The building first housed some bad ass kids who didn't appreciate the legacy of that building, but that has since changed.

If you've ever seen the ShowTime series the Tudors, the set interiors reminded me of school, minus the yummy actor Jonathan Rhys Meyers who made a very delicious Henry VIII.

Now I'll have you know that I almost didn't make it to this school, because I had my mind set on going to Erasmus Hall which was another Music High School located in Brooklyn. It was the only school that I knew of at that time where I could follow my dream of becoming a singer. Notable alumni would be Clive

Davis, Stephanie Mills, and Barbra Streisand. However, my mother said no to me going there because it was in the Flatbush section of Brooklyn which was a very bad area at the time. All I could do was cry, sulk and complain.

One day while still in Junior High I was talking to my guidance counselor, being very dramatical, of course, telling her how upset I was and that I hated my mother for not letting me following my dreams at Erasmus. An angel, she nonchalantly said, well why you don't try out for Music & Art. You're already in the Gifted & Talented program and that would help your chances of getting in. What type of school was it and where was it I asked? In her easy breezy way, she said oh it's another specialized high school where you can study music as a major, but you will have to audition to get in. She got me the application; I filled it out the same day and a few months later I was granted an interview and audition date.

I auditioned that spring. My father drove me from Brooklyn into the city and of course we got lost in Harlem. It was a bitch trying to figure out how to get up the hill by car. Yeah, ok that's what happens when you grow up in the BK. I was late and freaking out. Eventually we made it.

I sang the first verse and chorus of "You Light Up My life" by Debbie Boone. I was asked to find middle C on the piano, asked to tap out specific time signatures and rhythms, to sing major and minor scales and asked to sing back what was played on the piano by the accompanist. I had to wait the entire summer to see if I had made it in. It was the middle of

August when I got the letter saying I was accepted into this amazing sorority of gifted teachers and students. And yes we did study regular curriculum subjects like any other school but we were also a part of an elite club.

So here we were the last graduating class from the "castle on the hill." Here I am, dress on, hair done, a little lotion on the face, more lipstick and more mascara. All I had to do now was to walk across that stage at Avery Fischer Hall in Lincoln Center. After this moment, here is where my life of becoming a "star" would really begin.

The closer it got to graduation day the more excited I became. My inner voice kept asking non-stop: "what next? What do I want to do with my life? It was like a record that played over in my mind day and night. I knew I wanted to continue to study music in college. I knew that I wanted to sing or act or do both on Broadway, off Broadway, with a touring company, with a band, with a music group, on television, radio, it didn't matter. I wanted to have great adventures in my life and I knew the arts would be the catalyst for them to come true.

As a senior in high school, I had considered a range of colleges: I looked at some State Universities of New York like New Paltz. But, in my heart of hearts, I really wanted to get out of New York and wanted to go to the best college I could possibly get in to, in a different place so that I could experience other cultures, lifestyles and diverse types of people like the ones I went to high school with. Interestingly enough, my parents didn't even bother to come to the college open house events at school. Again, I felt that they didn't show up for me when I needed them most. I ended up going on my own that night. I did my best to bring up my grades after I fucked up my first senior year.

High school wasn't that hard, actually, in fact it was one of the best, most life changing experiences ever. I loved studying and singing Latin, Italian, German and French vocal music. That's how I began my appreciation of classical music. I undertook Music Theory, Composition, Music History, Sociology, English Literature, Gospel Chorus, Opera Workshop, Musical Theatre Workshops, and I got to do all of it with people who were like me, who had the same things in common and with people I genuinely liked and cared about. Oh and yes we did sing in the hallways in between classes. Yes, lunch was always a blast! Yes, we did dance, rap, and sing, out in the streets and on the subway. Yes, all of us were THAT damned talented.

Yes, I had to repeat my senior year because I was having way too much fun not going to classes. I knew that it might hurt my chances of getting into college so I went to summer school, and then attended night school. When I went to classes and studied hard, I could and did earn good grades. I was part of our cheerleading squad, drill team, I played volleyball, was in various choruses. I practiced for my music history exam and the SAT's for months.

Then came again, open school night for seniors. It was a chance to meet faculty from different colleges all over the country. For a second time, my folks didn't bother to come to the college open house event at school. Again, to my disappointment, I ended up going on my own that night.

I applied to three music schools. California Institute of the Arts in Los Angeles, California, Berklee College of Music in Boston, Massachusetts and Hartt School of Music in Hartford Connecticut. My admission letters slowly began to trickle in.

One came on a cold, wet, blustery November afternoon. I recall slowly opening the soggy 8 1/2-by-11 envelopes and trying to be ever so careful not to damage the life-altering information inside. When I saw the word "accepted," I felt like my dream had come true. I was going to California. Don't you know my mom said no because it was too far away and we had no family there at the time to keep an eye out for me. I thought, this is crazy, my parents didn't even take the time to come to school on college nights, they didn't bother to help fill out applications or help write my entrance letters and now they're saying I can't go? I was distressed. Then came the coup de grace, I was told there was no money for me to go to college. What? There was no money put away for me to go to college? I was devastated!

Then, the acceptance letters for Berklee and Hartt came. My parents weren't very helpful in the grants/scholarship arena or supportive in figuring out a way to make it work. There was no savings account, no college fund. They knew nothing about how to get academic scholarships but what really hurt was they didn't really try. My mom did inquire with someone at work about a government PELL loan for undergraduate students to help alleviate some of the costs in my freshman and sophomore years but due to both parents working I wasn't eligible for the maximum amount in federally subsidized student loans. What they wanted to give me wasn't going to be enough to pay for even my first semester. My cousin mentioned to my mother that maybe she could say that my dad wasn't living in the household to get more money but my mom said she wasn't going to lie. My mother made it clear that the $15-25K per year tuition and fees were far out of reach for our family.

They both had honest jobs. My mom worked at Morgan Guarantee Trust Company down on Wall Street and my dad worked for the Metropolitan Transit Authority. We lived in a middle class Brooklyn neighborhood. My father, who was old school, couldn't understand why after just studying music for four years in high school, why I wanted to go to college for another four years to study more music. I guess that's the thought process when parents don't understand their child's passion or calling.

The consensus was that our family had lots of other financial obligations at the time, so suffice it to say when all of my friends were saying goodbye that August, going off to various schools around the country to continue pursuing their art, I did not go. My dad made a statement of "the fun is over, time to get a real job." He suggested working for MTA and proposed that I take the test for a Token Booth Agent. You remember tokens, right? Anyway my heart fell into my shoes and my eyes glazed over and I said to myself hell no, I'm not working in a token booth!

After all was said and done, I was left with the only option; getting a job. But where? What did I know how to do? All I wanted to do was to become a singer and actress on Broadway! I don't think they understood the yearning within my soul to use the gifts I had been given. To work and live my life doing what I was so passionate about.

Chapter *Nine*

*...She wants to lead the Glamorous Life,
Without love-it ain't much-Sheila E.
Glamorous Life- WB Music Corp.*

And so here we are! It's 1985. I'm on my way to finding myself. This is the point in my life where I had begun to establish who I was and what I was made of.

It's February, VH1 has just debuted, Prince is on his Purple Rain Tour, Apple and IBM are the only two serious players in the personal computer game, compact discs had just arrived before the common term CD's were being used, although they were becoming popular, they still hadn't quite caught on yet. Mafia Boss Paul Castellano is shot on orders of John J. Gotti. Riots and protests continue in Townships in South Africa against apartheid policies.

Early on I made the decision to start auditioning, but needed the usual, headshots, sheet music, monologues, dance shoes, lesson, etcetera and my father was on my ass about not working or helping out with bills. So to appease him and not have to ask him for anything I got a job through my neighbor who lived upstairs from us. He worked at LaGuardia Airport in housekeeping. I took a job at LaGuardia from 10pm to 7am for a hot minute vacuuming the terminals and cleaning the bathrooms. This most certainly was not a glamorous life or my idea of fun but if nothing else, it without a doubt humbled me.

My new job was at Bloomingdales; this was more my speed and at least I could get clothes on discount and go to auditions in the city during the day. Because I was a floater at Bloomingdales, I got to work in different departments all over the store. I loved chatting with the customers and being around beautiful, luxurious things. This particular day I happened to be in the chocolate shop which was on the 59th street side of the store. My coworker said there's a guy here, says he stopped in to pick up your tape. I looked out the window. It had stopped raining.

And there he was. He was listening to this bumble bee colored Walkman and dancing around à la Michael Jackson. He had on a black leather jacket, underneath a red-sweater with a crest on it, and black slim high-water pants. He was what we would call light and curly. It appears that he was singing. People who walked by glanced at him for a brief second but not caring too much at least not enough for them to break their stride or lose focus on what they were doing, who they were talking to or where they were going. Why, because it was New York City. That's one of the things I love about NY. For the most part we New Yorker's are jaded and cynical because we've seen it all. It takes a lot to faze people in this town.

I said to myself well he's a little full of himself isn't he. He was eating up all the attention. My next thought was maybe this would be my big break. A few weeks earlier I saw an ad in the Village Voice that a Music Group was being put together and they were looking for a female singer. I placed a call and this guy named Secotine; the pronunciation is Sake-o- teen. I know! Ok, his real name was Kenneth but that's what he called himself. Who was I to judge? Anyway, Secotine told me about the other singer, his partner Daedalus. I know, yes, that was his real name too. I couldn't believe it either. I thought Daedalus as in Greek mythology Daedalus? The nerd in me decided to look it up and I was right!

Daedalus pronunciation, DEAD-DUH-luss, rhymes with bus. In Ancient Greek it's connoted as "clever worker" In Latin: Daedalos. Daedalus had two sons Icarus and Iapyx. Daedalus was a celebrated craftsman and architect. It was he who designed the Labyrinth for King Minos of Crete. Daedalus was an innovator. Before his time statues had their arms fixed stiffly to their sides; he created them with naturalistic poses; gave them fluidity, the power of movement. Daedalus consequently murdered his nephew who was also a builder in a fit of professional jealousy. Because of this homicide, he fled his native Athens for the court of King Minos on the island of Crete where he and his son Icarus ended up being imprisoned by his own creation. Are you seeing and feeling the drama of this family? I have to say this was definitely art imitating life.

Over time, other stories have been told of Daedalus. Daedalus is first revealed by Homer as the architect of a wide dancing-ground for Ariadne. The Labyrinth on Crete, was where the Minotaur (part man, part bull) was kept. The most familiar literary explanation of Daedalus' wings is a late one, that of Ovid: in his Metamorphoses (VIII:183-235) Daedalus was shut up in a tower to prevent his knowledge of his Labyrinth from spreading to the public. He could not leave Crete by sea, as the king kept stringent watch on all vessels, permitting none to sail without being carefully searched. Since Minos controlled the land and sea routes, Daedalus set to work to fabricate wings for himself and his young son Icarus. He tied feathers together, from smallest to largest so as to form an accumulative surface. He secured the feathers at their midpoints with string and at their bases with wax, and gave the whole a gentle curvature like the wings of a bird. When the work was done, the artist, waving his wings, found himself buoyed upward and hung suspended, poising himself on the beaten air. He next equipped his son in the same manner, and taught him how to fly. When both were prepared for flight, Daedalus warned Icarus not to fly too high, because the heat of the sun would melt the wax, or not too low either because the sea foam would soak the feathers.

They passed the islands of Samos, Delos and Lebynthos but by this time and having fun Icarus, forgot himself and began to ascend upward toward the sun. The blazing sun melted the wax which held the feathers together and they came off. Icarus then fell into the sea and drowned. Daedalus as a father wept, bitterly mournful of his creation of the wings. He called the land near the place where Icarus fell into the ocean Icaria in memory of his child.

Daedalus Winthrop Brooks-Smith had just as much drama in his family as with the famous Greek tragedy. His father was Derryck, born in the British West Indies. His family moved to New York in the 1950's, when he was about ten years old. He had a master's degree from City University and was either a teacher professor; can't remember which. Derryck was this brown skinned health nut who wore those 1970's style gym shorts. You know the ones that would be considered hot pants by today's standards. He wore these running shorts during the winter, summer, spring and fall. Even during special events he would dress this way and he would round out his ensemble with these timeworn beat up sneakers. He even showed up at one of my nightclub shows wearing exactly that.

Through his t-shirt you could tell he was fit and in pretty good shape from his biceps. I think he was an avid runner because his calves and thighs were well defined, ridged with muscle. He wore his black hair short and perhaps there were just a suggestion of some gray hairs. While his face was fine-featured and his smile disarming, at best he could be considered intellectual yet quirky and he could also be a bit of a jerk. Daedalus' mother was the beautiful spirited Etta and he also had three sisters.

So here we are present day! Secotine, Deirdre and Daedalus. All pretty unique names wouldn't you say? Wow I thought! This could make for a very interesting group. Heart pounding, I go outside and introduce myself. Hi I'm Deirdre. No, not Dee-dra! Yes D'- Ear- Druh! I hand him my homemade cassette tape. I said I hope it sounds good. Obnoxiously, throwing shade, he said well either its good or it isn't and chuckled. I cocked my head to the side and raised an eyebrow. It isn't a professional demo, it's me singing along with a couple of records, I stated. I quickly mentioned that Secotine said it was okay that I didn't have time to make a professional recording. Seeming a bit annoyed, he said 'well it will have to do.' Give me your number and my partner or I will give you a call to come in and audition. Two days later at around 10:00 pm I got the call. Hey, this is Daedalus can you come tomorrow to Harlequin Studios? My partner and I will meet you there at 7:30 pm. I said sure give me the address; uh huh, uh huh, okay see you then.

I was really nervous about my audition with these guys. What should I wear? Something cute, something sexy? Let's see, I don't want to look too cutesy, they might not take me seriously, and nothing too sexy. I didn't want to come off as being slutty. Let's try this short black skirt with dark tights, boots and a cropped sweater to expose just a bit of my stomach. In the style of one of my fashion idols, Jody Watley. There, that looks cool and funky with just a hint of sexiness. I wonder what their personalities are like. Shit! I just hope this isn't another wild goose chase.

I loathed living in Coney Island and I hated living in a two- fare zone. I took a dollar cab ride to the Stillwell Avenue train station. Shit, it was cold out here by the water. I can't wait until I move to Manhattan. This was one of my ultimate goals, to live in the city. That's where all the action and excited happened. All of the great parties and the fun people were in Manhattan.

I hated that we moved from Bed-Stuy a few years after I graduated, to Coney Island, Brooklyn. Coney Island, was at the edge of the world where the ocean meets land. God I hated it here! The only excitement that happened in Coney Island was a fight on the corner, or the police making a drug bust. I missed living in Bed-Stuy. At least we knew our neighbors and it wasn't a violent neighborhood or at least not on our block.

I ran up the smelly filthy subway stairs at Stillwell Avenue, hoping the train would be there but it wasn't. God I can't wait to get out of this shit hole. The smell was making me nauseous. Hotdogs, fish and chips, piss and grease. Two more months of winter and then spring would be here. Boy I can't wait. Just as I said this to myself another gust of wind blew so hard that it took my breath away. I got on the N train. Ahh! It was a car with the heat on full blast. I was the only one in the car being that it was the last stop before the train turned around to go back to the borough of Queens. It's was going to sit here for another ten minutes.

In the mean time I pulled out my nail polish to go over my nails. While waiting for them to dry I began to go over in my mind how I wanted to introduce myself. Should I be flirtatious, cool and laid back, very quiet or business like? Cheerful voice: "Hi I'm Deirdre", cool voice: "What's up, I'm Deirdre" or my aloof voice: "hey." Jesus, what was I going to sing? Fuck it I said to myself. I'll just be who I am and if they don't get it then so what. I'm not going to get all weird about it. In fact, I'm not going to think about it at all. I'll get there and let's see what happens. I closed my eyes to take a nap. I had at least an hour to 46th Street and Broadway.

    Just as I opened my eyes, I heard the conductor say the next stop 42nd Street. I laughed to myself. It's amazing how us New Yorker's can sleep on the subway but always wake up before our stop. The conductor recites his mantra, "Next stop 42nd street Times Square. Change for the Q and R trains the 7 and Shuttle, A, C, 1, 2, 3 Trains. Step in and watch the closing doors." I stand and walk over to the door. I see my reflection in the glass. I check my hair and makeup, run my fingers through my hair and blot my face to make sure I wasn't shiny. Everything is well in place, and I'm looking pretty damn good. The train pulls in with a squeal to my stop. I get off and make my way through the crowd to get outside. I pull out the address again. Hmm, 46th Street and Broadway around the corner from Howard Johnsons. That's only four blocks away. Good, because I'm so nervous I have to pee. I made my way down the street.

    There it was, Howard Johnson's. It orange neon sign lit up the entire corner. I made a left turn on 46th and saw the awning that said 203 Harlequin Studios. As I opened the door the smell of urine hit me. It was like smelling a bottle of ammonia for the first time. The smell stung my nose and made my eyes water. Facing me was a steep flight of stairs. I hesitated for a brief moment. I thought maybe I was mistaken.

Perhaps I had inadvertently come into the wrong door which was the Gaiety.

The Gaiety Burlesque Show, where men would go to watch male strippers and jerk-off. I thought is this it? Is Harlequin part of the Gaiety, where weirdo's and out of town married men met other men in private restrooms for more entertainment than was being offered at the show?

Mayor Giulliani eventually had the place shut down. I checked the address again. Nevertheless, slowly I walked up the dark creaking steps. At the top of the stairs you could see a faint light. I pulled opened the old squeaky glass door. The first thing I noticed was the smell; it was really musty, dank, dark and strange like that 90's television show "Twin Peaks". It had this creepy unsettling feel to it. Kind of like a campy B-movie horror film with eccentric characters. For the short minute it took my eyes to adjust, my first impression was fuck, this can't be it! It was like a Dante's Inferno for creative people. It seemed like a place where singers, actors and dancers went to die. It was as if it was decorated with furniture people had set out on the streets. It was dirty and run down and reeked of mold.

There was a woman who looked like she was in her 60's named Freddie who chain smoked at the front desk. Purportedly, she and her brother inherited the studio from their parents who were pretty big back in the days of the Ziegfeld Follies. Now mind you the Ziegfeld Follies were popular in the mid 1930's. Allegedly the studio was used by a lot of big name celebrities. Who? I couldn't tell you their names. Hi, I said to Freddie. I'm here for an audition with Daedalus and Secotine. With a cigarette dangling precariously out the side of her mouth, eyes squinting from the cloud of smoke that covered her like a crown, in her gravelly voice that sounded as if all she did was drink bourbon and smoke cigars, said they haven't arrived yet. So I took a seat.

The bizarreness of the place had me mesmerized for a minute then I remembered that I had to pee. Freddie pointed me down the hall to a bathroom around the dark corner. I passed a vending machine with discontinued candy in it. I found the bathroom and it had this eerie red light on the inside. Oh my god I certainly didn't want to use it but I really had to go so I made it quick and got out luckily without touching anything with my hands. I got back to the waiting area and watched as these peculiar casts of characters came and went. Some of these odd people were walking around getting coffee out of the nasty looking dirty machine, booking more studio time for $8-$12 an hour. Wow, the good old days.

In one corner I noticed an old cigarette machine where you had to put in change and pull the knob straight out and the pack of cigarettes would fall down into the tray below. Sitting in one of the dark corners I eyed these chairs with the stuffing coming out of them wondering to myself is this how all people start out? Cuz you've got to be fucking kidding me! Is this what you call paying your dues?

I looked at my watch; it was 7:45pm. Ok they're late. Strike one. Just then a tall handsome guy walked over to me and asked my name. He was a ball of frenetic energy that was teetering on the edge of spontaneous combustion. He acted as if he was about to explode. He spoke at a lightning speed pace and had a lisp. His energy was all over the place. He introduced himself as Secotine.

Yes, I know his name sounds a bit contrived! I know. What can I say? Deirdre, Daedalus and Secotine all sounded a bit over the top.

He said sorry I'm late; I was stuck on the train. I said, oh that's okay but in my mind I thought, mmm hmm this is already strike one, no one is on time. This was a pet peeve of mine.

Secotine said, I listened to your tape but couldn't hear you very well because you're singing with the record but from what I could hear, you have a really nice voice. Sec went on to tell me what he and Daedalus were trying to put together and what kind of sound they were looking for and so forth. Another guy comes in and gives Sec a hug and introduces himself. Hi I'm Ray Gordon, he shakes my hand. His energy was interesting; it was very warm and positive and he had a bit of a southern tilt to his voice. Are y'all ready he asked? Where's Daedalus? Sec said he should be here any minute.

I followed behind them in the dark hallway. We walked up another flight of stairs, down past some other studios where you heard people singing, tap dancing and reciting monologues at full volume. Ray opened the door to the room and there was one window and what looked to me like a 30 year old orange carpet. I happen to look up and some of the ceiling tiles were missing. It reeked of old stale cigarettes. It was the type of room where a really cheesy, grungy 1970's porn movies were filmed. Over in the corner were a few brown folding chairs and a brown upright piano. Covering all of the walls was this dreadful brown wood paneling. What kind of joint was this?

Ray sat down at the piano and started to warm us up with some scales. Then he started to play a song that Sec knew and Sec started to sing. It was a song by Ashford and Simpson. He kept apologizing when he got to a note and didn't quite hit it dead on. He kept saying he had a cold or a sore throat. This would be his favorite excuse for the entire time that I knew him. He was always off key and flat. Sec was the kind of singer that didn't retain his musical parts very well so he was always singing someone else's notes.

That's one thing I've learned, never apologize. It makes you look less talented and insecure. I remember on one occasion I was performing somewhere but had a cold. No one knew. After it was all over someone congratulated me on what a beautiful voice I had and I said oh my goodness, I must have sounded awful because I have a cold. That person said if you have a cold and sound like that then I can't wait to hear you when you're in perfect voice. Ray asked me if I wanted to do a song and I said okay. He starts to play The Greatest Love of All. Just when I was into the last verse Daedalus walked in with so much attitude trailing behind him like a haze.

Hello everyone, sorry I'm late. I brought you all some peppermint tea with lemon and honey. His vocal cadence was interesting in how he over pronounced his words as though he was reciting Shakespearean prose. I thought it was a bit much at first but soon realized he was for real. In fact, he was an actor studying at the Actors Studio so it kind of made sense. Actually, he was a triple threat. He danced and sang as well. He was sanguine in the way he walked. He was tall, slim, well-toned, lithe, long and lean.

 He stood at 5 feet 9 inches, had smooth café au lait skin, beautiful brown expressive soulful eyes framed by long eyelashes, chiseled cheekbones and curly black hair. I thought wow that was considerate of him to bring us hot tea. Perhaps he's not a jerk after all.

 In fact, his energy felt a bit mellow, boarding on melancholy. Was that you singing he asked? Eagerly I answered yes that was me! He said very nonchalantly, oh.

 What? Huh? Did he just shade me? What's with his fucking attitude? There was something about this guy I did not like. He was just as rude and arrogant as the day I first met him and meeting him again today trying to come at me, I said to myself, what an asshole! He was obnoxious, big-headed, conceited and loud. Inside I was all riled up! I couldn't get over his snobby attitude. He threw shade at me without blinking those beautiful lashes. I must admit he was very good looking. All the same, I was the wrong girl to mess with.

 We began working on our harmonies for "The Greatest Love of All" by Whitney Houston. At any rate, as the two hours of rehearsal went on we all were able to relax and let our guard down somewhat. Sec and I were laughing, joking and ragging on Daedalus more than we sang. I had to give Daedalus a bit of his own medicine and didn't back down from his snide comments or jokes. Next thing we know the bizarre looking phone in the room rang. It was this big black phone box that had no numbers on it to dial out but just the receiver and it was Freddie at the front desk saying that our time was up. As we said our goodbyes I said to myself, I really do like these guys. I would like to work with them. Let's see how this goes. Sec and Daedalus said they would call me and let me know what their decision was.

Honestly, I think I was the only one that actually auditioned but they had to make it look good so they made we wait. But hell, I was pretty, I could sing, knew harmonies, and was committed to rehearsing twice a week. Needless to say I got the call. I was in.

We began rehearsing in March, twice a week on Mondays & Fridays. Before I realized, it was already June and we were preparing for our first show.

At this point we had begun hanging out after rehearsals. Sometimes we'd go to BBQ's on 72nd Street or would go to Central Park to hang and smoke some weed. On a warm rainy day in May, Sec and I bought a cake and a bottle of champagne and we took Daedalus to Washington Square Park to celebrate his twenty-second Birthday. By the time we arrived the rain had stopped.

We found the perfect spot on one of the benches. We put one candle on the cake and sang

Happy Birthday. We used a plastic knife to slice the round vanilla cake with the light blue and white frosting. I'm glad one of us remembered paper plates and the little Dixie cups. Dae turned on his boom box; Sec lit up a doobie and passed it around. We ate, drank, and laughed so hard our sides were hurting. We were making fun of some of the people as they came into and through the park. Daedalus began offering strangers slices of is Birthday cake. As they took the cake they stayed and hung out with us dancing and having fun.

Weeks thereafter, the three of us continued hanging together after rehearsals. We had a talent show coming up in a few weeks that Ray had booked us for and we were excited about our first performance.

On a warm night in July after coming from rehearsal, Dae had his boom box that day to record our rehearsal. We were headed to the train station and was blasting Janet's "What Have You Done for Me Lately" singing and dancing as we walked down the street on Seventh Avenue through the crowds of people in Times Square.

And here comes this police officer saying turn the radio down, it was causing noise pollution. Me being a smart ass said to the officer, how it can be noise pollution in the middle of Times Square? This isn't a residential neighborhood it TIMES SQUARE! Daedalus and Sec, busted out laughing! And for my smart mouthed comment, the cop confiscated the boom box and gave us a $60 ticket for noise pollution. Of course, Sec and I chipped in

$20 each so Dae could go down to the police station, pay the fine and get his boom box back.

I was having one of the best summers of my whole entire life. I would go to work and then go to rehearsals at night. We ended up naming the group RareForm because during rehearsals we would throw sarcastic jokes and snarky comments at each other so easily that it would make a normal person cry but would make us laugh so hard that we couldn't sing. Ray was always saying oh lord y'all are in rare form tonight. But the name also signified our goal of wanting to be exceptional performers.

We'd go to different places to party and to watch these Vogue and Drag battles of the different Houses like the House of Omni, the House of Ebony, and the House of Chanel to name a few. Yes honey, this was way before Madge made it popular in 1990.

We'd hang and have fun until the sun came up on the weekends. Being that Dae and I lived in Brooklyn and Sec in Queens we often travelled back to the train station together after getting a bite to eat. Sometimes Ray would join us but most of the time he had other musical groups he was working with so he always had to cut out early. In the meantime I got to hang out with two of the most wonderful, interesting people I had ever met. It was cool because being the only female with three guys that loved music and singing as much as I did, were kind, funny and spontaneous was awesome. They respected me and treated me like a little sister. To me they were my brothers in all things musical.

It's funny how when you're enjoying life, ones' soul can be and feel extremely spontaneous. When I was around these guys my soul felt light, loose and home. This easiness drifted just like the wind through the trees and while this flow, our flow had a consistency, it's was never fully predictable. It flowed according to the indescribable possibilities we held within our consciousness.

Sec, Dae and I connected. We were linked by way of our love of music and the similar life experiences of the neighborhoods we grew ups in, family issues and our hopes and dreams. With that said, our relationships with each other slowly began to shift. Things between Daedalus and me began feeling a bit different. Daedalus would look at me in rehearsals and stare just a second too long. The energy between us was electric but I had never thought to ever take it any further because I didn't want to mess up our group dynamic. Secretly there was definitely an attraction between the two of us.

Our relationship with Sec moved to a different space as well. I became concerned about Sec because he had become a bit weirder than normal. His behavior was becoming more hyper. He was more restless and irritable than usual. There were a bevy of women that he was involved with. He was beginning to not know the music and always with the sniffles because of his 'cold'. I would catch him gazing at me in a peculiar way that felt intrusive. This was the beginning of the end.

Chapter *Ten*

Must be love
It must be love, talkin bout love
Must be love, It must be love, talkin bout love
Something's got me upside down
And I never been like this before
Something's got me goin in and out
And I never moved like this before...-Alton McClain & Destiny
"It Must Be Love" David Allan Stewart, Bob Geldof, Universal Music
Publishing Group, Spec-O-Lite Music, Writers:

The New Year finally rolled in. It was 1986 and we were back in rehearsals right after the holiday break. Sec had started missing rehearsals a lot more. We needed to have a group meeting about him being AWOL, not knowing the music and his unreliable behavior.

Little did he know that Dae and I were always on the phone for hours at a time talking about nothing and everything. More and more we were hanging at the Paradise Garage and the Danceteria together excessively. For some reason I didn't want to share this with Sec yet because first, I didn't want him to think Dae and I were making alliances against him and was somehow pushing him out of the group. Secondly, I didn't want to spoil things. Our bond was important to me. We all had so much fun when we did get together. So much so that we didn't have to think about the negatives that were swirling in our individual lives. We didn't have to deal. I wanted to continue to indulging in the carefreeness of us. I know it was selfish but I didn't want it to be different.

Then Daedalus started behaving erratically. It seemed as though he was depressed one minute and happy the next; he wasn't himself. One day in rehearsal he just blew up at everyone and left. I was so confused. Sec seemed a little perplexed as well. However, he still didn't know about me and Dae.

It's so remarkable. Looking back, in retrospect all of the signs were right there in front of him. Didn't he notice that when Dae and I kissed and hugged hello and goodbye it was just a tad bit too long? Did he not realize while all of us were at the club dancing, hot and sweaty, seeing Dae and me feeling each other up and kissing each other to the beat of the music that things were different? If he did he never alluded to it. Not that there was anything going on between Daedalus and me but when we were out dancing, we just got so caught up in the moment. Dae and I understood that dancing was your body's way of singing. Your body was just interpreting and expressing how and what a song made you feel in that particular moment.

Time seemed as if it was flying by. I felt like I was the luckiest person in the world to have these guys in my life. Who knew that following your dreams; better yet, that following your heart could feel like this? After speaking with Dae one night on the phone for what seemed like minutes I realized that it was actually two whole hours. I always hung up with that same familiar feeling of contentment and happiness; of love. Was this love? I loved him as a friend. It felt as if I had known Daedalus forever. That's how quickly we bonded. We talked about a lot of things.

Our upbringing, our challenges, fucked up things our parents did, what we wanted in life. We just flowed.

One weekend we went upstate to his school Bard College for a party and to visit some of his friends. Bard was such a beautiful place located in Annandale-on-Hudson, which is about 90 miles from New York City. The setting at Bard College was unlike your typical college campus. It's more like an enormous village spread out across 500 acres of parks and woodlands. The campus is serene, quiet and nestled close to the Hudson River and the Catskill Mountains. Travelling there during any time of the season was oh so beautiful.

One of the charms in going to a school like Bard was their semester-based academic calendar. For outdoor recreation, students could go horseback riding, canoeing, hiking and biking. I would have applied if this school was on my radar but at the time I was caught up in getting far away from Brooklyn and New York as I could. Seeing the campus on my first few visits, I believe I would have loved going to college there. Not only was the landscaping breathtakingly beautiful but most of the buildings were profoundly influenced by Collegiate Gothic architecture. Perhaps this is what felt good and familiar about the place. It had this reminiscent feeling of my high school Music & Art; "The Castle".

After seeing the lush vines of the Boston Ivy that climbed and covered the outer walls of the countless older buildings on Stone Row, I immediately fell in love with the atmosphere upon my feet touching those lovely grounds for the first time. The entire campus was magnificently manicured.

We walked over to Blithewood Manor where students were just hanging out on the great lawn communing and taking in the sun. When you come upon Blithwood Manor for the first time, you are at a loss for the right words to explain the majesty of the place. It originally sat on eight hundred and twenty five acres of land during the 1800's. At first look Blithewood Manor appeared large and dignified but this historic estate also had a charm and softness to it. It was comprised of a manor house, gatehouses, drives, the surrounding gardens, and the magnificent great lawn that could perhaps be compared to Sheep's Meadow in Central Park.

While we were waiting for some of his friends to show up Daedalus took me for a walk in the gardens.

Wow, the Bard Garden! It looked like a small Italian villa and it was designed to perfection. I remember the gray gravel stones crunching under my feet. There were vines and scrubs. There were lovely pink and white flowers that kept my eyes darting back and forth. There were these curious looking blue flowers and purple flowers; perhaps lilacs. There was so much to see, I didn't know where to look.

Regardless of whatever types of flowers they were, they produced a wonderful fragrance and attracted loads of bumble bees and butterflies to their blossoms. There was a beautiful fountain that added even more life and movement to the garden. The fountain created a soothing, peaceful energy. The friendly faced statues also caught my gaze. They echoed the sweet essence of the flowers that filled the garden beds. I remember seeing these gorgeous delicate white peonies that seemed delighted to be safe within the stone walls of the garden. Then. Then there was the piece de resistance. There it was; a breathtaking, awe-inspiring backdrop of the Catskill Mountains and the Hudson River.

    We sat down on the marble bench in the middle of this glorious place. While I was admiring the flowers that were in bloom and trying to take it all in, Daedalus leaned in and kissed me. It was gentle, slow and smooth. And there they were. The flutter of tiny butterflies in my stomach. He looked at me; smiled, grabbed my hand and led me back to the lawn area. I had no time to process the thrill of that first kiss.

    I was bewildered not only from the kiss but was baffled by the fact that when his friends finally did show up, he introduced me as his fiancé. This totally shocked me. No matter how flirtatious we were with each other, no matter how touchy feely we got when dancing at the club it never went any further than that. We weren't lovers. What the hell was going on? We had never even mentioned the word 'love' to each other. We just enjoyed being in each other's company, let each be who they were in any given moment and didn't judge. I had his back and he had mine that's all that mattered. Our friendship was unconditional. However, the sexual energy between us was there. Other people saw it and made little comments about it but we didn't talk about it or act on it.

After the party on campus we went back to his friends' dorm room where we crashed on the floor. He kissed me again and again I was a bit stunned but after all the drinking and smoking I wanted it to go further right then and there but it didn't happen. This began the 'dance'. He would push me away one minute and the next be all lovey-dovey. Things were becoming so muddled. I tried to check-in with myself but things felt out of sorts. My feelings felt totally opposite of what I felt the other night. Last week we were at the Garage and after dancing our asses off for hours we went up on the roof to cool off. He pulled me to him because I was getting a bit chilly and kissed me. We were both stoned so I didn't think anything of the kiss. Being in close quarters with people having fun, writhing under the cover of strobe lights and dancing to music so loud that it vibrated inside of your chest; I knew that this would never happen in the light of day when we were both lucid. When he let go of me he stared at me with those big brown eyes for what seemed like an eternity. I said what? What's wrong? He was a bit choked up but finally said that he was glad that we were friends, but that's all we could be and he didn't want to hurt me. I gave him a hug and said I too was glad we were friends, all the while thinking how was he going to hurt me? He was my best friend. I couldn't figure out what he meant at least not at that time. It felt like being on a rollercoaster and not knowing where the sharp twist and turns are. That night on the rooftop, at that moment I felt anxiety, fear, and helplessness wash over me.

What I know for sure is, sometimes the hardest part of a relationship, platonic or intimate, is walking alongside someone who is going through a period of sadness or hurt. They may be miserable for days, weeks, or longer. Lots of individuals break- up in their friendships or intimate relationships because they can't deal with someone who's always going through it. But if you're committed to the relationship, friendship or otherwise and want to see it through, be ready to be the cornerstone and warrior for the relationship.

During one of our late night phone convo's Dae was crying, severely depressed and talking about ending his life. I was so scared for my friend. He was drinking vodka and taking valium and was thinking about taking a bunch of other pills. After about an hour I was able to talk him into coming to Coney Island so he wouldn't have to be alone. He finally showed up around 1am and was in a very dark place. Although I was conflicted about some of the dynamics in our friendship, I decided to step back and just be there for him. To come from a place of understanding and help him control the dark troubled waters he was wading in.

We had this ritual where we would sit face to face, hold each other's hands and say to each other "tell me what you're feeling" but we wouldn't speak it out loud. When we looked into each other's eyes, time and space had no meaning. Sometimes twenty minutes would go by and we would just sit gazing into each other, letting the energy of what we were feeling, what we needed to say flow between us. This particular night while we were soul searching with each other, in the quiet early morning hours, tears began to pour. There were a whirlwind of emotions of hurt, pain, confusion and sadness. We wept. After about 15 minutes of our ritual, we both then began to laugh. No words, just laughter and then just sitting contentedly in the silence with entwined hands and open hearts. When we looked into the other's eyes, we saw ourselves in each other. The tears had released us back to us. Back to optimism and hope, joy and love. And in that relief the waters calmed within.

There was a special sacredness to our relationship that transcended anything I had ever experienced before and have never experienced since. We sat up and talked and watched the sun come up and then fell asleep. While I was still sleeping, Dae had gotten up to use the bathroom. Being that I was still living at home, my parents were horrified that I had let him stay over. I didn't care. Although I tried to explain the circumstances, I don't think they really ever understood that my friends' life was at stake.

Chapter *Eleven*

If I tell you, If I tell you now
Will you keep on, Will you keep on loving me
If I tell you, If I tell you how I feel
Will you keep bringing out the best in me
You give me, you give me the sweetest taboo...Sade
"The Sweetest Taboo" -Martin Ditcham, Helen Adu © Sony/ATV Music
Publishing LLC

On another occasion of us hanging out Dae expressed to me that he was so glad that I was in his life because I didn't judge him and the things he had done or been through. And that I was so open and loving and saw the good in him BUT he couldn't offer me more than his friendship in return. I was a bit crushed but at the end of the day he was my friend and I would still care about him. I told him I would be okay with that; us as friends. Two weeks later he shows up at my house one night without any notice. I opened the door and said oh my god what are you doing here? He said I had to see you! I invited him in. He said I need to tell you something. I said ok. We sat down on my bed and he just blurted it out. I'm attracted to you and I want to be with you and I love you! I couldn't wait until tomorrow and I had to tell you face to face. After the big confession he seemed relieved.

He got up and looked out the window. Here he was standing before me proclaiming his love for me. I was shocked and elated all at the same time. We hugged and kissed each other again and again. I grabbed my jacket and we went and walked the boardwalk down to the rides.

We played some ski ball, and hoops and talked some more. We headed down to the beach where he kissed me and held me and then wrote his name and my name in the sand surrounded by a heart. There was an electrifying feeling between the two of us that words cannot describe. That's when I knew, believed there was such a thing as a soul mate. We were soul mates. We would communicate without speaking. We read each other like an open book. We connected passionately on every level of being. Sometimes picking up the phone to call each other simultaneously, or feeling like we couldn't be without each other. On the flip side, our soul mate relationship wasn't all rainbows and unicorns either. Daedalus and I challenged each other like nobody's business. But what would you expect when a fire sign Sagittarian like me, mixes it up with the dual personality air sign Gemini like him. Astrology says that when Fire and Air get together, there can be a lot of inspired thinking. Fire helps Air find focus when scattered, and adds hopefulness to any plans hatched. Air can articulate the big picture for the impulse-driven Sagittarius, while the former keeps things from being all talk and no action.

Fire and Air signs are allegedly compatible since Fire needs Air to burn. So for the most part when

Dae and I were interacting in a healthy, well-balanced way, we would function like a hot air balloon, the inside flame lifting the balloon to heights it could never reach separately. But when we weren't; boy-oh-boy! Fire and Air; me and Daedalus. The two of us kept each other in stitches, opened the doors of insight and found new ways to surprise each other. This was exactly how it was between us but we also knew how to push each other's buttons very well. For example when my fiery temper was stirred and Dae's attitude started to bluster, there would be an explosion along the lines of a bomb detonating when we fought.

Now I'm the first to admit that as a Fire sign I'm driven more by my emotions. For instance, sometimes if I'm torn between logic and emotion we'll more often than not the latter side wins. Gemini's, on the other hand, are more driven by logic and are inclined the exact opposite way. So needless to say, if I was already burning hot in the temper department and Dae, threw too much logic at the argument, all it did was aggravate matters and make me burn even hotter. Although when necessary, he engaged the desirable logic that would diminish or cut my Fire's air supply. Thus there were many truces called or discussions finished later when we were both in a more calm state.

Despite what people might assume, just because you have found your soul mate doesn't mean it's always smooth sailing. The relationship always comes with its challenges. Finding your soul mate isn't going to always be Skittles and lollipops because life situations have a way of making sure of that.

However, the difference is that circumstances and difficult challenges is the reinforcement that becomes the glue that keeps you together through the difficult times and helps each of you become your most authentic self.

We evolve as people. At least we're supposed to. And to help us with that evolution is someone who pushes your buttons and aggravates you at first because they bring with them some of the more difficult lessons for your soul. That's how I felt about Dae when I first met him. I didn't like him. He was so jerkilicious! When we got to know each other we still didn't see eye-to-eye on every little thing, but we were on the same page where it really mattered. We shared the same goals and ambitions and wanted nothing but acceptance, love and happiness for each other and collectively.

It was one of the most beautiful June afternoons. The skies were blue, the sun was shining brightly. I left my house in run down Coney Island to make a stop at his place in Crown Heights. I fried up some chicken at his place and we bought some Champaign; a combination that rich socialites would trade in their pate and caviar for right? Daedalus and I loaded up the car with pillows and a blanket and set off to Washington Square Park. When we arrived around 4:00pm, the park was already crowded with jugglers, musicians, comedians and a great potpourri of interesting people.

We found the perfect spot by the playground. We pulled out the goodies, cracked open the Champaign and just enjoyed the day and each other's company. And last but not least a joint. We drank, smoked and started to make out. Other couples were all around us, making out in the grass too. The sun was going down. Things were becoming hot and heavy between us but we weren't ready to go back to Brooklyn yet so we decided to go somewhere else. Perhaps more secluded. At that moment, I had to go to the bathroom. I walked a couple of blocks to a restaurant. When I got back to the park Dae was all packed up to go. A couple passing by us stopped us to say how beautiful we looked together. I found it strange that people were always saying this to us.

It was around seven thirty. The goldenness of the sun was disappearing into burnished amber and gently fading away into the dusky, lavender, water colored sky. We laid there on the grass and enjoyed watching the beautiful sunset, then decided to make our way to the car. What was it about sunrises and sunsets with us? Was it the whispered promises that came with the night or the hope and promises that each new day would bring? All I knew was that enjoying sunrises and sunsets together made my soul always felt like it somehow expanded and that feeling always made my heart feel full.

We stopped at a store on the 72nd Street and West End Avenue, got some drinks, trail mix and some ice cream. We still weren't ready to go home so we drove around a little bit longer. We decided to go to Riverside Drive Park and hang out. It was now dark and the summer night sky was now a dark indigo that made the stars sparkle. After spending almost thirty minutes looking for a parking space, we were ready to make our way into the park. It was after ten o'clock at night and eventually we couldn't see our hands in front of our faces the deeper we walked into the park.

Undeterred, we continued on our mission to find the perfect spot. We stopped in an area where the trees were all around, enveloping us like two arms giving a hug. We chose a spot but realized we were not alone. There were other people in the darkness. I couldn't see their faces. Just then my nose led me to who was there. They were derelicts and bag people. We decided to keep walking. Then the perfect spot appeared to us.

It was on a hill covered with trees next to the expressway. The only thing that separated us from the speeding yellow taxis and cars was a wide metal guardrail. We lit up the rest of the joint. We talked about what a perfect day it was, how much we enjoyed hanging out with each other, how glad we were that we were in each other's lives. He kissed me gently at first and I kissed him back softly. We then kissed each other passionately. We began exploring each other's body as the kissing became hotter and heavier. He had already taken off his t-shirt and my blouse. After he peeled away my white laced camisole, there was no turning back, no interruptions, no mixed messages. On this balmy night, we slowly made love with one another. While he was not my first, making love with him for the first time felt sacred to me. Especially under the night sky, with the moon glowing off in the distance. The degree of intimacy and friendship between the two of us was without parallel and we finally got to celebrate it.

It around one in the morning. Sweaty and breathless we wrapped ourselves in our blanket, talking, whispering and then we snuggled together finally drifting off to sleep. Before sliding deliciously down into a peaceful slumber, I had a quick memory flash of that night on the rooftop at the Garage but it was gone as fast as it appeared in my mind. I was content. I was happy.

When we awoke it was almost daylight. The indigo sky was surrendering to purple hue of morning. The sun would be coming up soon. It was quiet in the park except for the birds singing their early morning songs. There were faint sounds of traffic in the distance but stillness in the cool morning air. We dressed ourselves and took a walk down by the water to watch the sun come up.

We talked. It seems we did lots of talking. Our conversations could go on forever but we were also comfortable sitting in the silence of each other. He kissed my forehead, kissed each one of my eyes. Subtly and delicately he touched my face and then kissed me slowly and deliberately. Until then never in my life had I known a kiss such as this, passionate and sweet. At that moment it seemed as if some essence beyond mere lust had forever bound us to each other.

Dae didn't always sleep well so when he woke up in the middle of the night or the wee hours of the morning he would call. He would call me at 2:00am or 6:00am and we'd talk, analyzing, contemplating, crying, sharing secrets, fears, anxieties, loves. We would discuss how rehearsals with our singing group felt. We both would watch the sun come up out our windows separated from each other by our individual neighborhoods. Him on his side of Brooklyn and me on the other side of the borough. To this day, I still love early summer mornings when the sky begins to cast away its purple haze.

    Here in the park. The sun finally made its debut. We ended up at our favorite diner the Waverly off of Christopher Street. We had a light breakfast and headed back to Brooklyn. We got to his house around 10:00am. We took a shower together and made love again which of course lead to another shower. I got out first and began to dry myself off and I looked up and he was standing behind me, starting at me with those brown eyes of his. We were both looking at the reflection of ourselves in the mirror. He held me and said how beautiful I was, how lovely my body was. He ran his fingers across my shoulders and commented on how beautiful my damp pecan brown skin glistened. Brushing my wet hair aside he softly kissed me on my neck. He cupped my breasts in his hands, letting his long dancer's fingers caress them. Saying to me what beautiful babies we would make.

    I turned to him, kissing his gleaming wet chest. He pulled my chin upward so that our lips met. He looked into my eyes, smiled and said I love you. Right then and there he had my heart. It was a divine moment in time. No matter what happened, this day would be one of the most beautiful moments in my life. I found myself staring out of the window. The sun seemed to burn more brightly, the clouds moved through the atmosphere like great wings against the sky. The air was sparkling. Every blade of grass seemed to shimmer with its own light. I saw myself mirrored in Dae's eyes and I felt beautiful. He took me into his bedroom where we made love again and ultimately fell asleep in each other's arms. When I woke up he had fixed lunch even though it was almost 4:00 in the afternoon. We had tuna out on the little terrace off of his room. We were laughing and making jokes about each other's mothers. God it felt so good to laugh again. I didn't realize how long it had been since I was over wrought with laughter. Daedalus had such a wicked sense of humor. He could be sarcastic and viciously sharp-witted at the speed of light. He kept Ray, me and Sec laughing all the time. His laugh would begin as a chuckle and get bigger and louder. His laugh could get you going so you couldn't catch your breath. He kept me laughing until my sides hurt and the tears where streaming down my face.

The next few weekends we went back up to Bard to hang out. This particular weekend, when we got back, we stopped in Brooklyn Heights to get a bite to each. He was kind of quiet at the restaurant but I just thought he was exhausted from all of the partying. We went walking on the Promenade and then back to his place. He tuned the radio on and then we made love and fell asleep. When we finally woke up, we wrapped ourselves in a blanket and sat out on his little terrace teasing each other as usual and rehashing the weekend.

In the midst of my giggling I noticed that he wasn't laughing anymore. He had this lost, helpless look on his face. I asked what was wrong. He took my hands in his and asked me not to speak until he was finished. He took a deep breath. I could swear he broke out in a bead sweat. And that's when he said it. Daedalus, told me that he was gay and that's what he meant when he said he didn't want to hurt me. I was speechless for what seemed like an eternity but it was only 2 minutes later. I remember the watch on his arm reading 5:07pm. This was the day, at 5:07. The day the bomb was dropped on me. What? How did I not see it?

I was searching for the words, the right words. But what were the right words? I was shocked, confused. What does he mean he's gay? What? He continued on. Me, I was in a stupor unable to form any intelligible words. Him telling me that he had only been with two other females in his life. One was a childhood friend at the age of seven and the other was with his therapist that he had started seeing at the age of 14 years old. What? He had sex with his therapist? Ok. That was so wrong, in so many ways.

He spoke about us and how much fun he's had being with me, how he was able to talk to me about anything and how he was allowed to be himself, to be free with me. He could talk as loud as he wanted, we would both sing and dance in the street, and even pay a stranger a compliment without the other getting jealous or feeling insecure. He said he wanted to tell me earlier on but was afraid to. He felt that he had to say something because he really loved me. He said he would understand if I wanted to end it right here and now. What? What?

The voice inside my head was saying what the fuck! WHAT THE FUCK? After being rendered mute for what probably seemed like infinity I got up, went inside and got my cigarettes. I went back outside to suck in some nicotine and try to process all that had just been said.

Being the intuitive person that I am, I needed a minute to check in with myself for some otherworldly guidance. My intuition had never let me down and had served me well in my continuous mission to finding myself, my truth and underlying meaning of things in my life. At first I couldn't get a gauge on what it was I was feeling. But as my elders use to say 'get still' and this is what I did. After a couple of hours outside on the terrace by myself chain smoking, I went back inside.

I sat down on the bed where Daedalus was. Face to face, we stared at each other eye to eye for about a minute, holding hands not saying a word. Just letting our hearts say and feel what needed to be said and felt. The higher self me felt nothing but pure love and I didn't want it to end. Who was the one that said love makes you do strange things? Then and there, we made love again. I didn't care. I loved him and he loved me.

It's ironic. When I first met him that day at Bloomingdales my evaluation of him was someone who was egotistical, smug and conceited. To sum it all up a real asshole! It was like he was always "on" always performing. I could never have someone in my circle like that I mused. It seemed as though he had a chip on his shoulder and acted like the world owed him something. And so, who would have ever thought that he'd turn out to be really compassionate, giving, sweet, sensitive, fun, witty, intelligent and beautiful person. I mean I'm normally a good judge of people. I got along with mostly everyone with the exceptions for those who were malicious to others because of their race, sexual orientation or gender. With that said, I always removed people from my life who were not open and inclusive to everyone.

Riding home on the subway the next day I kept thinking, he's gay? He's gay? Oh my God! Oh shit! He's gay!

I had gay friends and knew people from my childhood who were. I went to a performing arts school for Christ sake. After all, I was a musical theatre kid! I thought maybe he's mistaken and he's bisexual. But no... he said he was gay. What do I do? Who do I talk to about this? Do I say anything to anyone? How would they perceive me? I don't want to be judged. But I love him. Oh shit! How could I not see it? After my long two hour train ride, I got home and took a long hot shower to try and clear my mind and find that voice in me that would tell me what to do.

That voice inside me said, "You can't worry about what others will say." "YOU have always followed your own heart; YOU have always listened to what your intuition tells you." This was crazy! Crazy because my gut feeling was saying go for it; experience this life while you can. Do what feels true for YOU.

Daedalus and I continued with our nightly two hour phone calls, dance clubs, hanging out down at the pier and being together. One day I got a call that he had been in a car accident coming back from Bard.

The car was totaled and he was okay physically. He walked away from the accident with a little scar and intact but was devastated because his car represented freedom for him and for us to go where we wanted, when we wanted.

About six weeks later I realized my period was late. I waited and waited yet nothing. Another two weeks had passed and I knew I had to tell him. I actually told him over the phone. He was shocked and ecstatic all at the same time. I was relieved. He wanted to be a father. He made a doctor's appointment for me down on Court Street for me to get a pregnancy test. We met up, and went into the appointment together. I was nervous when the nurse called my name. They took some blood and made me pee in a cup. I went back out to the lobby with Daedalus to wait for the results. After about 20 minutes the nurse confirmed that yes, I was about 7 weeks.

Pregnant. Daedalus immediately hugged and kissed me and said we're going to have a baby! I was still in shock and for a split second wanted to jump out of the window. With this Cheshire Cat smile on his face he asked me how I felt. Seeing the joy in him made me feel a lot better and actually made me feel a bit calmer. Other than having headaches and wanting to sleep I was fine. We went to a spot in Brooklyn Heights to celebrate our good news and then went back to his place. When I woke up from a nap he sat on the edge of the bed, took my hand and gave me this blue turquoise ring as a symbol of his commitment to me and our baby and asked me to marry him. Oh shit! It was decided that we would keep the baby. We enjoyed the rest of that amazing, scary, happy day. Back at his place, I was worried about telling my parents and how they would react. He said not to worry that it would be ok. He kissed me so tenderly and we made love. Afterwards he laid his head on my naked belly, whispered something to the baby, closed his eyes and we both fell asleep.

No Ordinary Love

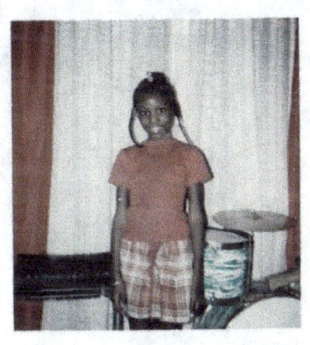

Look at all those 45's

Practicing my curtsey

ME & MY BEAUTIFUL MOM

No Ordinary Love

After graduation I was so ready to take on the world!

I started modeling soon after.
Here are some shots from my very first photo shoot.

No Ordinary Love

My hair looked like a Hersey's Kiss

No Ordinary Love

We were so young...

Daedalus W. Brooks-Smith
Singer-Actor-Dancer

Singer, Actress, Model

Daedalus had such a wicked sense of humor. His laugh was infectious; bringing tears to your eyes and making your belly ache from laughing so hard.

No Ordinary Love

Daedalus loved celebrating his birthday

No Ordinary Love

Memorial Day Parade New York City-Fifth Avenue

No Ordinary Love

We were special guests at the Apollo. Of course Secotine was cutting up back stage while we were trying to get dressed.

No Ordinary Love

No Ordinary Love

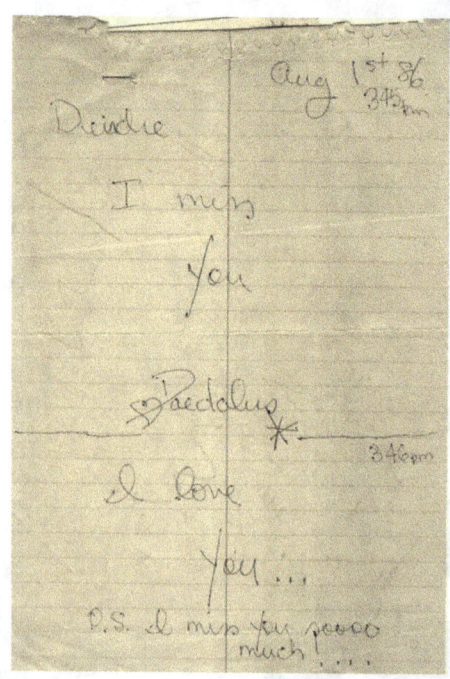

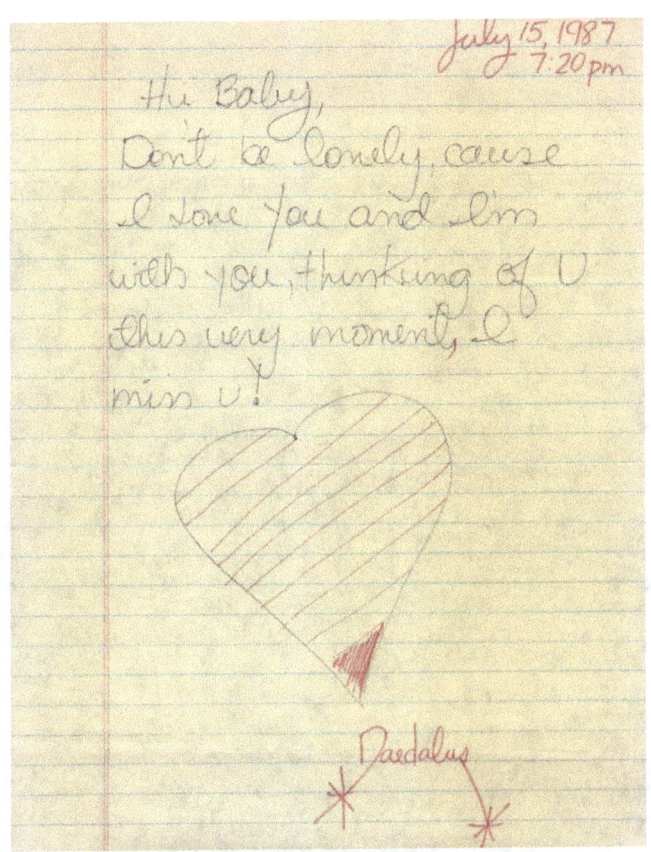

Getting ready to hit the stage...

Bard College Campus

Bard Garden

No Ordinary Love

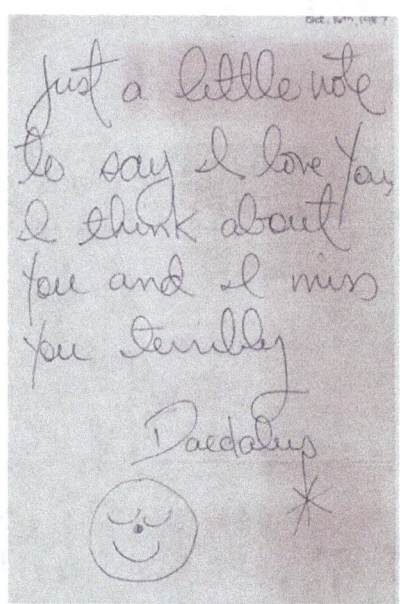

Waverly Diner-Our meet-up spot

No Ordinary Love

No Ordinary Love

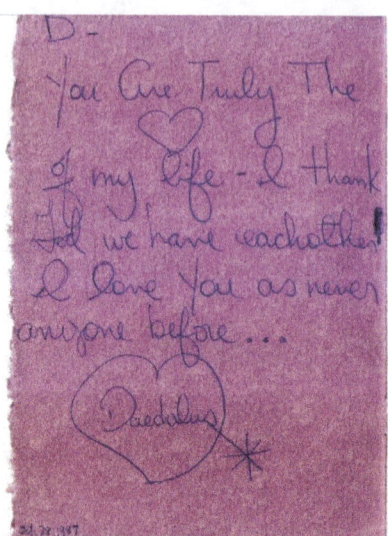

Only you . . .

A lot of people know the surface side of me,
the side they see while I'm working
or just going through the day . . .
But there's another side of me — an inside —
that people never see.
It's a part that's full of a thousand thoughts;
a part that embraces love and cherishes friendship,
a part that understands without need for words,
a part that has yearnings and desires and prayers.

The inside of me has so many moods
that the outside never shows.
For once in my life, though . . .
I trust someone implicitly
and I care about someone in a totally
   understanding way . . .

Our last holiday together in North Carolina

Daedalus and his sweet mom threw me a Birthday Party AND with 22 candles!

No Ordinary Love

No Ordinary Love

Me at Broadway Baby
This was my first attempt at singing without him standing beside me. I dedicated this show to him.
My heart was so heavy.
His parents were so sweet and came to offer support.

One of our hangout spots- Washington Square Park
Among our other places around town, it's still one of my most beloved places. The park brings me comfort especially when I'm missing him.

And so began my year of firsts without him...

Mom gave me a puppy to lift my spirits. I named her Bailey.
The jacket I'm wearing was his.
I wore it until if fell apart.

Summer wasn't the same without him there.

Sec was late for the photo shoot

I had pretty much given up on singing because I always ended up crying. It became too hard because there were so many memories and feelings attached to the music. Ray convinced me to join his gospel group the Lighthouse Singers. (Ray G. top center, Secotine B. far left, Wanda K. lower left, Jane middle, Me, John C., far right)

No Ordinary Love

Slowly I began to find my smile again...

I even went back to modeling, acting and eventually singing

DEIRDRE

No Ordinary Love

No Ordinary Love

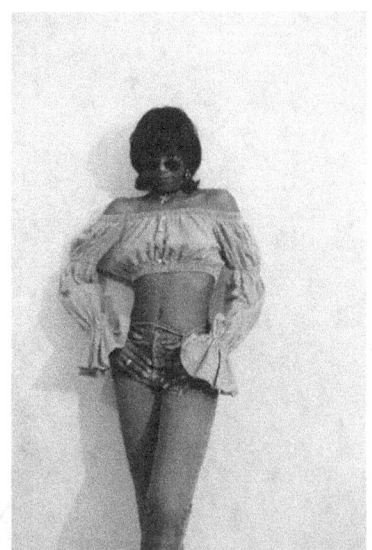

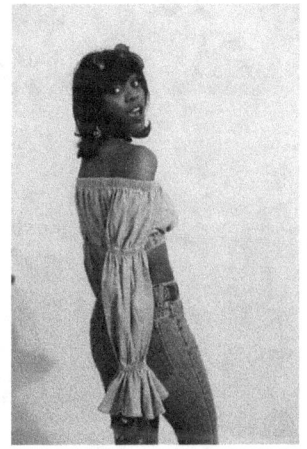

No Ordinary Love

No Ordinary Love

No Ordinary Love

In the studio working on my jazz album

Performing with the Jazz Great David Durrah (far left)

Deirdre L. Hall-Songwriter

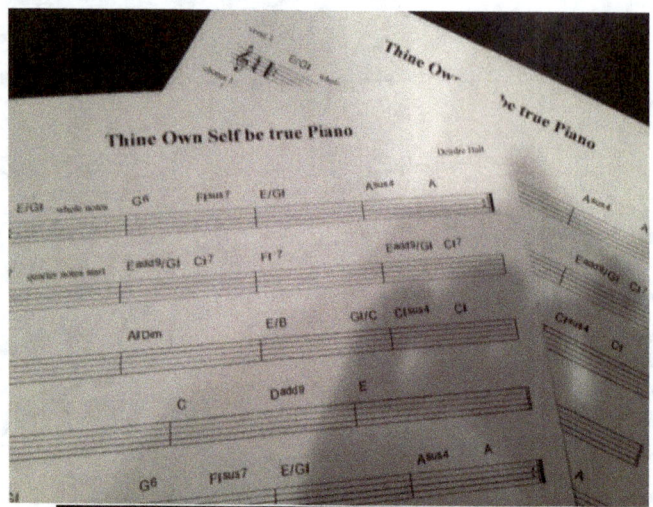

This is what the book first looked like. I began working on NOL after having vocal surgery in 2015. Its's hard to believe it's finally being birthed into the world.

My first time reading of excerpts from No Ordinary Love at City College of New York to creative writing students. I was so nervous, I wore Daedalus' scarf for good luck!

Guest Author appearance!

Professor Sweeting-DeCaro invited me back as a Guest Author at the City College of New York to read from No Ordinary Love, and speak about my writing process to her students. What a blast! I'm forever grateful.

All images ©1965-2020 Deirdre L. Hall
All Rights Reserved

Chapter *Twelve*

I have a tale to tell
Sometimes it gets so hard to hide it well
I was not ready for the fall
Too blind to see the writing on the wall
A man can tell a thousand lies I've
learned my lesson well
Hope I live to tell
The secret I have learned, 'till then, It will burn inside of me.-Madonna "Live To Tell"-Madonna Ciccone, Patrick Leonard ©Warner/Chappell Music, EMI Music

I still hadn't gotten up the courage to tell my mom but I knew it would have to be soon. But in the meantime we enjoyed our little secret. We were both so happy. Making plans to get an apartment of our own hopefully with the help of our parents. I got a call from him a few weeks later to meet him at our spot in the village, we needed to talk and that it was serious. The whole hour and a half train ride I kept thinking what could it be? Is he breaking up with me? Did he tell his folks and they said not to have the baby? Did he have a change of heart? What could it be? He said don't worry, we'll get through it. That's what he kept telling me and so like a mantra I kept repeating it to myself. When I arrived at the Waverly he asked me to sit down.

He began by saying that he loved me very much. The waitress came over and gave us menus. After a long pause, he then spoke about a test he took for this virus when he was out in California and the results were back and he was torn between knowing and not knowing. I said, knowing what? What are you talking about, some virus? The hairs on the back of neck stood up. At that moment a feeling of impending doom crawled from my head to the bottom of my feet. I had to get some air, so I got up and walked out of the diner. I was standing outside the diner like a marble statue. I couldn't catch my breath; my heart was pounding in my ears. I was paralyzed.

While in high school I had just starting hearing about this fatal, dreadful wasting disease. Physicians in Southern California and New York City began seeing a pattern of unusual infections and cancers such as KS or Kaposi's Sarcoma and PCP also known as Pneumocystis Pneumonia in young and otherwise healthy homosexual men. It was also called G.R.I.D. an acronym for gay- related immunodeficiency disease or the "gay cancer." Oh my god! I began to cry. I started pacing up and down the sidewalk saying "Oh my God, oh my god." Oh my God! I yelled out.

Someone stopped to glance over their shoulder. Noticing that I was okay they kept right on walking. He came outside for me. When he looked at me I saw a shadow pass across his face and the tears welled up in his eyes. Shaking, I said what are you saying to me Daedalus? What the fuck are you saying to me? Oh my God. No one survived this, this virus. Nobody! We both stood on the sidewalk embracing each other and sobbed. What made you go and get tested I asked him? He said he wasn't feeling like himself and was having night sweats and swollen glands.

We both shed a lot of tears outside on Sixth Avenue that day. Through those tears and talking we came to the conclusion that it was better to find out the results. There was a chance the results could turn out to be negative right? Pulling some tissues out of my purse I wiped my eyes and blew my nose just as a lady with a baby stroller walked by. That's when I remembered. Oh no, oh my god, I'm pregnant! I was carrying his child-our child. This realization hit me like a ton of bricks. I began to weep again almost falling to my knees. He had to find out because I was carrying our child.

I remember reading back in 1981 a woman named Elizabeth Glaser who got infected from a blood transfusion while giving birth to her daughter Ariel. Ariel contracted it though breastfeeding. In 1984 her son Jake contracted the infection in utero. Sometime in 1985 Ariel got sick with a series of illnesses and the whole family decided to get tested. Elizabeth and her son Jake where diagnosed as HIV positive while Ariel had advanced AIDS.

Like a crazy person I went searching for information. I was looking for treatment information. I kept telling myself that- I've got to learn about the various opportunistic infections and all that was known about this virus. I feel like this was the first time I truly, categorically had any concept of what was happening. I had no close friends and family that I felt

I could turn to. No one I felt I could trust. I had no one to guide me in "What to do?" There was no one to walk me through what was going on or help me prepare for what was to come.

What I did learn was as many as 80% of people died within three years of getting their diagnosis. Doctors were saying that although it is likely that AIDS is due to an infectious agent, it is possible that the virus has an incubation period of up to two years. AIDS could be passed through sexual partners or through blood transfusions. But no one knew for sure. People thought HIV could be transmitted through saliva or tears. The public was fearful about whether mosquitoes could transmit the infection. People didn't want to kiss you on the cheek. People certainly didn't want to have sex with you. All that I had read up to that point was that this disease was very isolating and demeaning. It was an awful way to live. Those who had contracted the virus died a lingering death. Is this what I was to look forward to? How does someone prepare for something like this? Dae said the medical establishment in California kept the results up to a year in case we changed our minds about knowing the results.

All I knew was if his test was positive, this was a death sentence and only time would tell how long he/we would have to survive. If I kept this baby, how long would I have to watch my child, my first born die? This was going to be a long battle and I'm not sure if I'm ready for a fight like this. Am I strong enough? Then another revelation it hit me. Was I infected with the virus? This was my worst nightmare. I didn't want to die. I didn't want him or our baby to die. What would my mother say? Do I tell her? I couldn't tell her! Not yet!

Weeks had passed since we found out I was pregnant and I, we had to tell our parents and make a decision soon. We weighed all of the options. Not a lot was known about the virus. There was a big chance that the baby would be born positive. What about me? There was a strong possibility that I was infected with the virus too. I kept thinking, I will have to bear the death of my lover, my friend and my soul mate. To follow, I'd have to witness the birth and death of my child. This would be too much for me to bear and I think I would lose my mind.

Should we bring this child into the world with the possibility of him or her being infected? It would be eight months of pure torture. Then I found out that an infant could become infected before birth or through breastfeeding. This usually happens if the pregnant woman first becomes infected with CMV or cytomegalovirus (sī-to-MEG-a-lo-vī-rus), during the pregnancy. What if we were both positive and the baby was not? Our child would grow up without the very two people who would love him/her the most. What if all of us had the virus? From what I knew about HIV, it was all tied up with sex and desire, a basic human need but it was also entangled with shame, discrimination, and fear. Dae and I cried a lot. We went back and forth. We changed our minds over and over. Eventually, we made a decision. Our first step, we would wait to see what the outcome was from his tests said first so we placed the call and left a message.

Finally, the call was returned along with his results. The test disclosed that he was positive. He did have the HIV antibodies in his system. Daedalus was HIV positive. He had the HIV virus. I had no words. I was shaken to my core. I was frightened and inconsolable. After his diagnosis, came the next step. We painfully decided that to terminate the pregnancy would be the right choice.

So, there we were one week later on the subway to Queens. The morning started out like any morning that we'd meet up with each other except that I felt tired, drained and terrified. Here I was moving through the world with unspeakable sadness and anxiety. Now, I've always heard other girls back in my old neighborhood on the block in Bed-Stuy talk about how many abortions they had and how many more they would get if they got pregnant again. I would look at them in horror. Jesus fucking Christ! How did I get here? I followed all the rules get through high school, waited until I was 18 before, I started having sex. I acted responsibly while dating Robert, using protection and birth control. Now here I am. In a life-threatening situation, which is causing me to terminate the life of my baby. Which may cause me to lose my own life, and lose my lover and best friend.

The entire train ride to the clinic I kept seeing his bright and smiling face at the doctor's office the day we went to take the pregnancy test. Being told it was in fact positive. Him saying, "I can't believe I'm going to be a father." Rejoicing and giddy he took me to an ice-cream parlor around the corner from the doctors' office in Brooklyn Heights. To celebrate he ordered the two largest ice-cream sundaes they had. Remembering how easily we got caught up in the excitement of it all.

At the Planned Parenthood clinic, the counselor jarred me back to reality. Miss Hall? Miss Hall? She was asking me for the umpteenth time if I was sure I wanted to go through with this; that I could change my mind if I wanted to. I looked down at the floor and contritely nodded my head yes. I thought of Daedalus out in the waiting area. Just then a nurse came out to get me. I kept asking her about all the different probabilities and numbers of possible outcomes, telling her what I had read and researched. I guess I was hoping she would say something different. Something that I had not read or a study I had missed that would be the perfect way out of this desperate situation. Like a scratched record, I kept replaying over and over the nurse saying to me there was not a lot of data and there would be a big chance that the baby would be infected and she also recommended that I get tested as soon as possible. The nurse brought me to another area of the clinic where I was to undress.

I was changing out of my clothes ever so slowly and she knocked to make sure I was okay. Once I had on the surgical gown and socks I was led into the cool blue room, my legs felt like cement. Time began lapsing into slow motion. Sitting on the edge of the table. Being asked to lie down. Asked to put my feet into the stirrups. Asked to scoot down. Tears begin falling down the side of my face. The nurse rubbing my hand. The anesthesia mask placed over my mouth and nose. The nurse rubbing my hand. Asked to count backwards from 100. Nurse rubbing. I was going under. I was crying and going under. It felt like my heart was shattering into a thousand pieces. Anguished for our child who would never have a chance, who we'd never get to meet. Nurse rub-b-ing... Gooo-ing un...

Daedalus was there when I finally came out of the anesthesia. We were both heart broken. Meeting me outside in the waiting room, after it was over and done, I could see that his eyes were bleary from crying. Kissing me on my forehead, he kept saying he was so sorry. I kept saying I was so sorry. He said I love you and wiped the tears away from my cheeks. Taking my hand in his we got back on the subway and went back to our piece of paradise in the Village, our home away from home.

At the diner, he ordered and fed me some chicken soup, being that it was the only thing that I could keep down. He took me home, got me in bed and left. I woke up and felt compelled to write him a letter.

Wednesday 11:55pm
Hi Daedalus,
How are you doing? Okay I hope. I was lying here thinking about you. Where you were and what you were doing, hoping you'd call but you didn't. I'm sure that you're well aware of how hard it is for me to

express what I'm feeling verbally therefore this is why I'm writing to you. You always told me if I couldn't say it to write it down. Dae, first and foremost I wanted to tell you that I love you! With all my heart and soul and I hope you know that I would never hurt you intentionally but intentional or not it seems that I have and I'm truly sorry. As of yesterday you could probably say we've been through a hell of a lot together. Some bad, 98% good. Yesterday was one of those bad times for us. For me it was one of the worst days of my life and I'll have to live with it every day until I die. I know you wanted to keep the baby. I'm sorry that I put you through that. You have to believe me! I'm sitting here trying to fight back the tears and I feel really awful. Because you are HIV positive I didn't see any other choice. Daedalus, what I'm trying to say is that I've caused you enough pain and I don't want to hurt you anymore. The thought of me causing you pain is too much to bear. I couldn't live with myself if I did. That's why I've decided not to stay in your life anymore. I'll just keep out of your way so you can get on with the good things in your life and right now I'm not one of those good things. You won't have me around to screw things up for you. If it weren't for me getting pregnant, me wanting to terminate the pregnancy which led to pushing you to the point where you needed professional counseling, your life would be better. When we first started seeing each other, I didn't think I would care for you as much as I do now but that's the way things happened. I know you're going away soon and I can't blame you but please don't leave feeling disgusted with me. I

> *know you're angry with me. I'm angry with me. So is God. I just hope you can find it in your heart to forgive me. I hope God can forgive me. Each day I'll think about you, about us, the good times we had and I'll never, never, ever forget.*
> Loving you Always & Forever-Deirdre

I didn't talk to him for over a week. I couldn't. I wouldn't talk to him. He wrote me back a letter or more like a note.

> **August 1st 1986**
> 3:45pm "Deirdre I miss you."-Daedalus.
> 3:46pm I Love you. I miss you so much.

I finally called him and he talked about how much he missed our late night calls and his best friend. He began trying to convince me into coming down to North Carolina to recuperate. His mother was a nurse in one of the best hospitals in Raleigh, North Carolina. He thought it would be best for me and for the both of us. He suggested we go and visit her for a while at least until I got better. I thought this would be a good chance to run away from all of this, but not so good because that meant that I had to tell my mom. There was no way she would let me go out of state without telling her why first. He got the plane tickets one week later and I still hadn't told her I was leaving and why. The trip was coming up in a couple of days. The day before I was to leave I knew I had to say something. I played out all scenarios but none seemed appropriate. I sat in my room for a bit and with all the courage I could muster, my heart beating inside my head, I told her that I was pregnant and had just terminated the pregnancy but I didn't tell her why. I cried and she cried. She said she had a feeling that's what was going on with me.

Very depressed, sleeping all the time, tired, reclusive… She said she was so very disappointed in me. She then began to yell at me. How come I didn't come to her before I made an important decision like that? How could I be so stupid and careless? Then she said I had to tell my father. She was so upset with me, she told me to get out of her sight and went to bed. God, if only I could tell her why I made this decision but I couldn't.

Around 11pm, I called Dae to meet me at the subway station at his house in about an hour or so. I wrote my mom a note, packed a bag and left. Dae was there when I got off of the train. He took me back to his house and we stayed up all night crying, talking, feeling ashamed of what we did and of letting our parents down. We cried for what we had lost or should I say gave up, for each other. I also cried because I was so scared I was going to lose him.

The next morning was a wet, bleary day which was perfectly appropriate for the depressed mood we were in. We caught our flight and arrived two hours later in North Carolina. His mother Etta was waiting for us. She took us out to where she parked, put our bags in the trunk, then gave me a big hug and said things would be okay. Oh how I needed to hear that. As she hugged me, finally I was able to exhale, thinking oh how I wish it to be so because I was exhausted mentally, emotionally and physically.

Once we got settled at her house I decided to take a nap but it took forever to fall asleep. I kept thinking about my mother finding my letter. I did leave the address and phone number to where I was hoping that she wouldn't call. To my surprise, she didn't. His mom and I talked; she prescribed some antibiotics and other medication and nursed me back to health. During this time Dae and I got to really grieve our loss, sharing all the things that we wanted for ourselves and for each other and with each other. A month had passed. September was here. We both arrived back to New York. He went back to college upstate. I went back to my job, both of us trying to get our lives back on track.

We were both feeling so guilty and still trying to process all that had happened with us this past summer. The sorrow we both felt changed us and things between us.

November 25th, 1986
Hi Daedalus-
If you have a couple of minutes I'd like to talk to you just to let you know how I feel at this moment and time. Well, what can I say that I haven't said to you already? I love you very much. More than you could ever possibly know. I'm glad that you are in my life. I value our friendship tremendously and I wouldn't dare do or say anything that might jeopardize that. I know you're still hurting from this summer, so am I. There's not a day that goes by that I don't think about us and what we used to be to each

other. Yes, I do miss the good times we use to share. Finally I can even admit that I do miss you having your car because it was the nucleus in the midst of our happiness and fun times. I guess I feel kind of trapped. Do you? I also miss RareForm. I never told you but I had always wanted to be a part of a singing group. To finally be accepted; me, my talent, flaws and all. You know I've gone through most of my life feeling left out, never really a part of something, out of place and having to pretend that I really didn't care one way or the other whether people liked me for who I was, what I looked like, or the color of my skin. But you know what? I did care! And I still do. Maybe that's why I became so addicted to you because you accepted me for me. You just never turned away and for that I thank you! I wish that I had kept the baby because I see how O.T. has managed through the years with Demi. I feel I could have managed somehow, someway. But then there's the virus. It's very hard for me to deal with your sisters being pregnant at the same time. When you first told me about Kecia, I said okay fine because I didn't know her that well. But when you told me about April I was shocked, jealous, angry, hurt, happy and sad all at the same time. That's quite a lot to deal with emotionally don't you think? To be completely honest I really don't like to be around April sometimes simply because of the way that she treats you in not wanting you to touch her or be around her because of your HIV and because it just hurts so much. This is one reason why I don't sleep well at night because I'm constantly thinking about the termination. With each passing day I think about it. When I see other little babies or kids I hurt. When I see little toys or baby clothes I hurt. But you know *what? In my heart I truly, truly believe that we would have made great parents because that life was conceived out of the strong and pure love we had for each other. Dae, if this is too painful for you, I'm sorry but I want us to be totally honest and open with each other. You have helped me grow mentally and emotionally. I've learned so much from you. You are so right about a lot of things and now I see. When you hold me, kiss me or even make love to me it's such a beautiful, overwhelming feeling which sometimes scares me.*

I'm still trying to accept the fact that you just want to be friends though sometimes it's kind of hard and confusing. You see, I thought friends were just friends. No touching, holding, kissing or anything. Even when we first started hanging out together, with us we were always a little more than friends but not quite lovers yet. It's very hard for me now to suppress my feelings for you but yet at the same time wanting to share them and show them and not wanting to scare you off or make you feel like I expect things from you. I'm trying so hard. Do you realize we've been "together" as a couple for about 7 months? I feel that maybe we're over the worst part and that we have a lot to look forward to. I will be your friend if that's what you want. I will support you in whatever you do always. Thanks friend for being here for me!-Deirdre

Ray wanted to know what was going on with the group. As a band, were we still together or was it over? Dae had begun to isolate himself from us. I had already begun auditioning for other groups. Sec was done and was doing his own thing. Daedalus knew we were moving on. He then wrote a letter to both me and Sec.

> *This is a letter to two of the dearest people in my life who have stuck by my side through all of my trials, tribulations and torment. I love you. I want you back in my life. I have truly missed US. I have counted my blessing. RareForm is one! Can we truly unite? I'm ready are you? With renewed faith and love, Dae. - December 2, 1986 1:40am*

Chapter *Thirteen*

I Hear Your Voice Now, You Are My Choice Now, The Love You Bring
Heaven's In My Heart, At Your Call I Hear Harps, And Angels Sing
You Know How I Feel
This Thing Can't Go Wrong
I Can't Live My Life
Without You
I Just Can't Hold On, I Feel We Belong
My Life Ain't Worth Living
If I Can't Be With You
I Just Can't Stop Loving You
And If I Stop ..Then Tell Me Just What Will I Do
'Cause I Just Can't Stop, Loving You-Michael
"I Just Can't Stop Loving You"- Michael Jackson MiJac Music ©
Sony/ATV Music Publishing

Happy New Year, it's 1987. Really? There was nothing happy about this New Year. It is 34 degrees outside right now. Wish I could have brought in the New Year out dancing with two of my favorite people but at some point you just can't hold on so tight. You just have to unfold your fingers and just let go.

January 8th was our last rehearsal as RareForm. It just wasn't the same. Dae went back to school but wasn't feeling well and he was scared. I was petrified but I was always trying to be positive and give him encouragement, love and care. He sent me a card that read;

No Ordinary Love

> *Your hands have held on to mine and soothed my tears away. Your heart has brought me joy- and taught me to believe in myself. You are a special human being and I love you.*
> *Daedalus- February 6, 1987*

He was beginning to feel a bit better and was able to start school again. In between classes he sent me a funny card that said "Love or Confusion?" It had a man walking his dog and the dog was hugging the fire hydrant, obviously in love. Inside it read "make that Love AND Confusion." He wrote;

> *I saw this card and I thought you'd enjoy it. I registered for two courses so far... things seem ok to good. I might be changing to a dorm on main campus. Hope all is well with you. Thanks for the package.*
> *Love Daedalus- February 1987*

Finally, on the 20th of March there had been the approval of a new drug called AZT, however you had to take about 30 pills each day. It was found to be extremely unpredictable and caused severe side effects and long term use sooner or later lead to viral resistance. Daedalus was already having complications from his HIV status. His T-cell count was low so he went back to the doctor for more tests. His next set of tests results was positive.

He now had full blown AIDS. It began with the diarrhea, swollen glands, and then the night sweats. While away at school came the change in his appetite and the weight loss. Through all of this I stuck by him because that's how much I loved him and him me. Yes we were having our difficulties with each other and fighting this evil disease but I kept saying that we'd beat this thing. Boy was I so naïve. Nevertheless, I began educating myself about AIDS and seized all the information I could find.

The HIV infection destroys the CD4 T-Helper Cells. The formal diagnosis of the transition from HIV to AIDS is usually confirmed by CD4+ T cell counts and also the level of HIV RNA in the blood. When a person's CD4 levels drop below a certain amount; which was decided by your doctor or health advisor, this would determine when a patients treatment could begin. Then came the numerous hospitalizations, the infections, the PCP (Pneumocystic Pneumonia), the brown and purple KS (Kaposi Sarcoma) lesions. Add to that the Toxoplasmosis, HIV Encephalopathy Tuberculosis, Non-Hodgkin's Lymphoma, Peripheral Neuropathy, Herpes Simplex, Candidiasis, Cytomegalovirus.

I made trips upstate many times to check on him and to try and take care of him; making sure to bring with me some of his favorite snacks like fresh fruit, Ginseng sodas, spike, herbal teas, peppermint soap. He had always been a bit of a health nut and was very conscious about most things that he ate. He took his vitamins habitually and was an avid juicer.

He had such a beautiful dancer's physic body so he was already long, lean and toned. He kept talking about the dance classes he was going to take next semester at Bard and how we were going to travel and sing together just me and him. This broke my heart because I knew he was in denial. I didn't know what to say. I didn't want to pretend but I didn't want to be mean to him and take away what hope he had.

How is anyone especially a young person who's bright, talented and by all accounts has their whole life ahead of them supposed to come to terms with their own mortality? I think slowly he was unraveling and was having a nervous breakdown. On this particular visit with him I noticed he had lost a lot of weight. His once lithe, muscular body was failing him. He couldn't even wear regular shoes anymore so he was always in slippers.

Then came the constant arguing about silly petty things. My heart saw it for what it was; fear. He was trying to push me out of his life. I'm so happy I didn't let him. I remember us going to see Anita Baker at Radio City, and he was looking gaunt and pale. People were staring but I didn't care. I held my head up and everyone who looked at me I looked directly at them straight in the eyes. My choice was made. I would be by his side until the end.

I'll never forget our last beautiful, normal time together. It was upstate at Bard during a long cold and snowy winter weekend. When he picked me up from the bus I saw that he had gained a few pounds back. He even had a bit of an appetite and was still relatively healthy. This time he was staying off campus. It was a huge white old-style farmhouse way back up on a hill between these apple groves. It had already snowed a few inches from the day before and snowed earlier that morning so the entire property was already blanketed with fresh snow. It was peaceful and tranquil. Why does the world seems a bit quieter when it snows? For me it felt like a splendid retreat where you could be one with nature and luxuriate with the one you love. That day it was cold and dreary and the snow had started to fall again. We stayed in this beautiful old house and hung out by the fireplace in the stone kitchen. When there was a pause in our conversations you could hear the stream that ran underneath the floor of the kitchen. That is how prior owners of long ago use to keep their foods cool. There was also a fireplace in his bedroom and this is where we stayed by ourselves the whole weekend nestled together. I decided to make us tuna casserole for lunch. We sat in the kitchen and talked. We listened to some music and reminisced about our rehearsals and summer. He kissed me and things became hot and heavy. Just then another student who was also renting a room came in and startled us. We jumped up, fixed our clothes and had our lunch. As the day folded into the evening, we ended up having a petty argument so in an effort to give each other some space; I went to write in my journal that Dae had given me as a gift.

March 1st 1987.
Well I'll be going home tomorrow but I don't really want to. These 5 days were wonderful. I still can't believe I'm here. Spending time away from Coney Island is just what I needed to re-coop. The concrete jungle was beginning to make me feel weary and worn with all its noise, pollution and nasty ass people. It's such a wonderful change of scenery. No tall brick buildings, or tall

skyscrapers, no car or bus fumes; tall green pine trees, land, space, fresh crisp, clean air. No little streets, only highways, open space and clean roads littered with snow. Being here with Dae in this big homey, old house ahhh. I love him so very much. I wonder if he truly believes that. His illness has put a great strain on our friendship/relationship. There's not a day that goes by that I don't say to myself how lucky I am to have Dae in my life. I count my blessings. Thank you God! Right now we're trying to give each other some space and at the same time wanted to spend every moment we could together.

By the time night fell, we had both apologized to each other. He lit some candles, turned on some music and we undressed each other and we laid in bed, our naked bodies pressed close to one another. There was nothing sexual, just pure intimacy, pure love for one another. We both cried, I held him all night long, never wanting it to end. Not wanting any of this to be really happening. Knowing that this would probably be the final time we would get to lay with each other like this.

His dad came up for the day. We all went to a poetry reading. My last hours there, we all talked about life and how we wished things were different in so many ways. Dae and I started singing this song by Brenda Russell, "God Bless You." It started to snow again. My shuttle bus was about two blocks down the road. I was relieved because my hands and feet were becoming numb. But I was sad to leave him. He kissed me goodbye. Told me he loved me very much, not to worry that he'd be alright. How I hoped for it to be true but in my heart I knew it would be the last time I'd see him halfway healthy. It was very windy and cold so he had this rosy glow in his cheeks. They put me on the bus which dropped me off about a mile from the Annandale-on-Hudson metro north stop back to New York City.

    I felt as if I were leaving a piece of my soul up there at Bard. Nothing could ever ease away the fear that crept up on me, stalking me from the shadows of my mind; the anxiety churning within me. My panic began swelling like the strings on a violin in a sad love song.

Chapter *Fourteen*

...Who's callin' the shots
One of us must make the peace
To have or to have not
The fire has got to cease It's a war of the heart
It's a war of the heart
It's a war of the heart...-Sade
"War Of The Heart"- Stuart Matthewman, Helen Adu © Sony/ATV Music Publishing LLC

March 3rd, 1987
Dad makes me so angry sometimes. I feel like balling up my fist and punching him right in the mouth! He had some nerve to ask me how come I didn't tell him I was going upstate to see Dae. I didn't bother because he would only lecture me about something I did or didn't do and why I was going. And besides what did it matter I already told Lila (Mom) where I was going. He was never interested in what I did or went before so why start now. He said I was wrong not to include him on my whereabouts. Is he joking? When I tried over the years to make him a part of my life he always had something to do like hang out with his buddies and drink or talk about the bills he had to pay. He hasn't said yes once in years. He said "I don't want to be a frog to be fattened up and thrown to the snakes" What the hell kind of metaphor is that? He's always thinking someone is using him. I think

he's really paranoid. Now he wants to play daddy?? It's a little too late for that. In fact 20 yrs. too late. Why start now?

I found a card for Dae with the most beautiful poem by Susan Polis Schutz which captured exactly what I was feeling. It's titled:

"Do You Really Know How Much You Mean To Me?"

>Sometimes I wake up
>in the middle of the night
>shivering from fright
>feeling empty
>feeling nothing
>because I think about
>how it would be
>if you weren't here
>And then I wonder
>if you really know
>how very much
>you mean to me
>how incredible
>I think you are
>how you are
>a part of all my emotions
>how you are
>the deepest meaning in my life
>Please always know
>that I love you
>more than anything else in the world

Dae: This card just about says it all… Just letting you know how much I care and I will always be here for you. To stand by you, in good times and bad. Get well soon!

> *Because there's so much we haven't done yet. And when your days seem their darkest, always took to the sun for I will be there shining brightly with a smile. I Love You! But remember God loves you most of all. Deirdre-March 1987*

Daedalus was back in the hospital. It was like being on a roller coaster. He would get sick, go the hospital, but then he would get better. This time he developed pneumonia. Time to get back into the ring and fight!

I found out the family reunion was happening this summer but I'm not sure if I want to go because the pedophile that I'm related to would be there, and I hate him for what he did to me. The last time I saw him, he pretended as if nothing ever happened but I will never forget.

I sang last night and people told me I sounded great, but I don't think so. Tasha the drummer was hitting on me the whole time. What will I have to do to make her understand?

> ***March 18th, 1987***
> *Got a note from Dae on a piece of plain notebook paper that said "Hi- I love you. Daedalus*

> ***Sunday March 29th-***
> *I'm feeling kind of ok... I spoke to Sec today. He and O.T. broke up again. He says this time it's for good. Haven't seen OT since she invited Dae and me out to her place in Staten Island. Right now I'm sitting on the beach looking out into the ocean. It's so cold. I wonder what Duedalus is doing right now. I guess I should call some therapists*

> *tomorrow. I've been speaking to Denise and able to get a lot off my chest. I told her that I thought Dae overdoes his illness. I don't think it's true but I'm not so sure sometimes. I told her Dae wants to get married and have kids, lots of them. Denial...I hope they find a cure for the AIDS virus. I'm feeling so alone right now. Should I call Dae? He doesn't want me to see him until he's out of the hospital.*

> **March 30th**
> *I just got off the phone with Daedalus. He called collect and then wanted to speak with Mom. He told me he told her that he was "in the life" and other things. Uggh I hate him! He had no right to do that without talking to me first. Then he started on wanting to know about my sessions with Denise and what we talk about. He asks me do I want to come to see him in the hospital. And I say to him, didn't you say it was best not to see each other until after he was out of the hospital and well again? It's getting to the point that I'm beginning to dislike him so much and I don't want his friendship anymore. I don't know what to do.*

When I close my eyes I try and see the best of Dae. I use my mind to feel his energy and send to him my positive energy. I think of how much I love and care about him. I allow these feelings in my heart to build up. I imagine these emotions flowing from me to him, in the form of a beautiful energy. I am gently offering this love energy to him.

Tuesday March 31st 12:10am-
Feeling sad, depressed, confused. Anxious to talk to Dae. I'm trying to understand him. I know he's not dealing with things very well. He's using his illness to manipulate me and others around him who care. He probably doesn't realize that he may have put my relationship with mom in jeopardy. How many mothers expect their daughters to get involved with someone who's bisexual/gay and dying of the AIDS virus? I'm not exactly sure of what he told her. I spoke to Denise today and she promised me that she would not discuss our sessions with Dae. Denise did say she spoke with his doctor today and he says that Dae is becoming very anemic but it's because he doesn't eat. And it's easier for Dae to create and deal with anemia than to deal with the HTLV virus. She said Daedalus is acting like a 4 year old so I have to treat him as such and to try to talk to him in getting some therapy because emotionally he's not well. And when he says that you're acting irrational and can't deal with things he's really talking about himself.

I hope he calls me tomorrow because I miss him so much. Friday is my first session with Susan. I hope she doesn't charge me a lot of money because I'm just getting by financially and still looking for a job. I'm still worried that mom is disappointed in me. I didn't plan this relationship with Daedalus it just happened. Believe me when I say that I wanted the baby so badly. But how do you explain to your mother you had to get an abortion because there was a possibility of the baby being infected with the virus. I'm still trying to decide whether or not to get tested to see if I'm positive. I'm so afraid. I wish someone could give me the answer as to what to do. I'm

so scared because I haven't done anything with my life yet and I don't want to die.
Sometimes I feel like dying so I won't hurt so much. I don't know who I am or what the hell I want or who I want or what I want from that person. Why am I here? Is my life going to get better or worse. I'm sick of playing these games with others and myself. I just want to be me, the real me. Who is the real me? Dae is treating me like shit and I could be infected with a deadly disease that could kill me. I love him!
Do I really? I have this bump on the inside of my mouth that won't go away.
...My world came to an end then you brought it back together again. Now there's no way I can go on without you. (Go On Without You- Shirley Murdock). Dear lord Jesus, help me to get through this, I don't know if I can go on. Give me the patience and the understanding to deal with this. Why does music make me cry? It's so amazing to be loved; I'd follow you to the moon and the stars above. There's nothing better than love, what is the world could you ever be thinking of...(Luther Vandross) Think I'll just sit here and cry, maybe I'll feel some relief.

My system was on overload. I was dealing with dizziness, loss of balance and light-headedness every day or so it seemed. The world was spinning too fast. My world existed of extreme fatigue. Feeling like I'm turned inside-out. Who was it that said crying is just the release of resistance? It's just a letting go of the emotional debris. Well, Pandora's Box has been opened. Perhaps there really is strength in tears.

Chapter *Fifteen*

These dreams go on when I close my eyes
Every second of the night I live another life
These dreams that sleep when it's cold outside
Every moment I'm awake the further I'm away-Heart
"These Dreams", George Martin , Bernie Taupin, © Universal Music
Publishing Group

Friday April 3rd
I'm sitting here at Harlequin Studio waiting for everyone. I got here early. I went to my therapy session today. Susan is ok. I told her everything about my past and what's going on with me in the present. (Do I have a future?) She says that I'm not crazy but I do need more counseling. Her fee is $65 hr. and I don't even have 65cents. I don't think I'll let her counsel me. I hope I can find someone with lower fees and a women who is Black!!! I don't think I'm going to go to the family reunion. (Maybe) if Dae can come with me. I hope so. I spoke to him this morning. He's going to have a CAT scan Monday. He sounded so much better than when I visited him at the hospital. I don't like that hospital 1 single bit! It looks old, run down and the nurses and orderlies couldn't give a damn one bit about their patients. I prayed so hard last night and through all my tears I think GOD heard me.

Dae's dad stopped in to see him so when I called he answered the phone and said Dae was on the toilet. I asked him some questions because the doctors wouldn't tell me anything because I not related to Daedalus and he said "oh but you are..." It made me smile inside and out. But then I asked myself do you really want to become a part of THAT family?? The question still remains...

If Tasha is coming to rehearsal tonight I hope she doesn't keep staring at me. How come she can't take a hint that I don't like her like "that" and don't want to get involved with her? She makes me feel uneasy. I hope she finds a girlfriend soon. Sec should be here soon. I wonder if he's spoken to OT since they broke up. I think Sec wants me because when he hugs me or looks at me it's not in a friendships sort of way. I certainly hope not. Daedalus & OT would be hurt tremendously and I don't think I could do that to them especially Daedalus.

Well it's almost time for rehearsal to start. I hope it's a good one because I can't stand when insecure singers like Jane, Gloria, Wanda, etc. come in with their fucked up attitudes!!

Saturday April 4th

On my way to Gloria's house for a band meeting. I hope it doesn't take too long. Daedalus called me this morning. The conversation started our just fine and he sounds much better. His family came to see him yesterday. I was surprised to find out April came being that she and Athena are so paranoid about catching AIDS from Daedalus. I remember Dae saying that she, April doesn't even want him to touch her stomach to feel the baby kicking because she's scared that the baby might become infected. Boy does she have some nerve when she's got secrets too. Lillian called today to let mom know she was throwing Tonya a baby shower April 11th. Thank god I have to perform so I have an excuse. It seems as though everyone I know is having a baby. I want one so bad. Chris told me Roy said Annette left town because she's expecting also. It all seems too much for me sometimes and I'm constantly having dream about me having a baby. What does it all mean? When I got off the phone after having a disagreement with Dae, I went back to sleep. I had a dream that I had 2 girls the oldest was about 2 yrs. old and the other about 8 months. They were both light skinned and had dark curly hair just like Dae. They both loved him so much. The youngest had big beautiful brown eyes just like me and she was so pretty and funny. Then in the dream Dae & I were staying with my grandmother and his father. Suddenly I was in a bank with my mother. It was where we both worked as telemarketers at the bank on 73st & Broadway but in the back down the stairs is where Dae and I lived. All of a sudden this guy who was about 19 yrs. old came into the bank with a sawed off shot gun. I ran behind one of the desks and tried to hide. He began shooting everybody. Then he found me hiding and shot me but for some reason I only got hit in the shoulder. I made believe I was dead so he wouldn't shoot me again. The scene startled me because there was a girl who knew him and she was screaming and crying "don't kill these people, don't shoot them" but he didn't listen. The bank shoot-out scene began again. This time it was a 12 yr. old boy who came in the bank and tried to shoot us but for some reason this white man stopped him before he could do any damage.

While this was going on I somehow crawled to a door that led to the back of the bank. Someone who knew the combination had opened it for me and we both crawled in and there was Dae & Mom and my 2 little girls there waiting for me. All of a sudden I'm at a college in NC which was very similar to Bard. There was lots of chaos and students running everywhere. 3 black students from Africa were looking for a place to hide. So Dae and I hid them in our house.... I don't remember the rest because the phone rang but I wonder what it could all mean.

Sunday April 5th 2:35am

The meeting turned out okay. I kept thinking about death, Daedalus and having a baby. The more and more I hear about babies, the more I want to get pregnant. I wish financially I could afford it. If I could I would do it in a heartbeat and not think twice about it. But by whom Daedalus? There's always that chance that the baby will get the virus from either one of us and I don't know for sure if I'm positive or not. And who knows maybe I can't ever have another baby being that I terminated this one. March 15th would have supposed to have been my due date. Which means the baby would have been approximately 21 days old. I think it would have been a girl. Lately I've been having dreams about me having a baby and as I recall in all of those particular dreams the babies have all turned out to be girls. I hope Daedalus gets better... I hope the both of us get better mentally, emotionally, physically and financially because I don't know how much longer I can wait. I'm yearning for a child and this feeling is getting stronger with each passing day. I hope GOD gives me a 2nd chance and

> *forgives me. I remember someone saying that conceiving a child is a gift that GOD gives to some people and gives others talents like singing and dancing. This smells like total bullshit! I feel so tired. My mind is in a ball of confusion. The best thing for me now would be sleep. Sometimes I don't want to because I will dream about violence, death, babies and Daedalus or hidden evil forces. Well let me get ready for bed, smoke a cigarette and try to think out some of my confusion and Dream. Happiness, evil, violence, future, me, Daedalus, babies, death me happiness, evil future, violence, Daedalus......this is what my thoughts feel like inside my head; "Mass confusion. Mom just said to move my clock up 1 hour. Is there really enough time????*

Was it Albert Einstein who said "time is just an illusion?" That the separation between past, present, and future is only a misconception. Please, can I move time back to before Dae got sick? Can I change the present state of where we are right now? All my dreaming about death and babies, maybe it's preparation for what's to come in the future.

"*There are three times; a present time about things past, a present time about things present, a present time about things future. The future exists only as expectations, the past exists only as memory, but expectation and memory exist in the present.*" -St. Augustine

> **Sunday April 5th**
> *Dae will have his CAT scan tomorrow morning at Northern Dutchess Hospital in Rhinebeck near Bard. He called today. We argued as usual. I told him it was over.*

Was that the right thing to do? He wants us to go to therapy together. I'm not so sure. I told him he's pushed me too far. Demanding things from me and others. He says "I can do that because, they can give him what he needs. He's so full of himself and arrogant that I feel like killing him sometimes. The other day I told him if the medicine was making him sick, if the food was terrible; if his diagnosis was taking too long then do something about it. He said He didn't have the strength to fight. Denise said that most of the time when Dae thinks he's getting his way, in actuality, the doctors, nurses, whomever was going to let him in the first place. Being that I said it was over between us, now he says he's going to tape his mouth shut and listen to me. I think it's a goddamned lie. He would say or do anything. But what gets me is when I said I would pick up my stuff from his house, he said fine. I wasn't ready to throw in the towel but he let me go through with it anyway. How come he doesn't fight for me, our love? That day in the village, when he broke it off with me I said to myself that I wasn't going to let him go without a fight. Was he willing to fight for me? NO! I wonder why? I didn't feel anything after I told him he takes me for granted all the time by expecting me to deal with everything he's going through with a smile. Being there for him when he needs it, running errands for him. He takes my love for him and tries to manipulate me with it by saying things like" YOU SHOULD" do this, WOULD do this if you love me or cared anything about our relationship and what we both had together. He said I think I know everything. I said cant I feel this way if I want to? He said I was ignorant about lots of things. I asked ignorant about what. He says he's not going to list them. I told him just because I don't speak on or about certain things doesn't mean I don't know. I'm sure he didn't even hear me. It's funny I said you only hear and remember what you want to remember. I could bet my last dollar that I could ask him about this conversation we just had and he could only tell me what HE said or doesn't remember and how his illness has an effect on his memory or that he can't help it. When I was pregnant and was feeling nauseated but didn't know why, how many times did he baby me and try to take care of me. Sure he brought me food, soup and made small talk and then left. He wasn't by my side as much as I have been by his. Sure he was concerned and made me go to the doctor. I think Dae uses his illness for love and attention and to make people feel sorry for him and want to take care of him. If this is not true then how come I feel this way? What gave me these feelings, not unless it was true? I would really like to know.

Dae spoke to mom last night, says he told her he was sorry and was worried about me, that I couldn't deal with things like his illness, the abortion and him getting sick again. All he thinks about is himself and believes that the world must revolve around him. What makes him think my worries are of him and his illness all the time? It's all so weird and the scary thing about it is I still love him and wanted to have his baby. Why, why, why?

Song "Always" is on the radio: ...Girl you are to me all that a woman should be and I dedicate my life to you always...Dae I will love you so for always!

Little did I know that people who are facing their own mortality begin pushing the people they love away in the disguise of arguments, breakups, aloofness and distance but what they really want and need is compassion and empathy.

Chapter *Sixteen*

...If you're lost you can look and you will find me
Time after time
If you fall I will catch you I'll be waiting
Time after time...Cyndi Lauper
"Time After Time"- Cyndi Lauper, Robert Hyman © Sony/ATV Music Publishing, Warner/Chappell Music, Inc.

April 9th 3:30am
I just spoke to Dae about 2 hours ago. Things must be looking up because the last time we spoke and then tonight we didn't argue or hang up on each other like we've normally been doing. I miss him so much and I know that he loves me but do I love him? And if so how much do I love him. Sometimes I feel like I do but lately I haven't felt anything at all. I did mention couples therapy to him and about what I felt and how I felt. He says I'm picking out all of his imperfections and he doesn't like the way that feels. Good, Good, Good! I'm glad. Because that's partly what he's been doing to me. Can I really accept him for who he is and vice versa?
Daedalus:
Love me for me
Honor my opinions and ideals
Respect my judgment and feelings
Understanding my way of thinking
Patience to let me grow at my own pace

Support not domination of my music career
Listen to me not only with your ears but with your mind and heart
Freedom
Fun & Joy
No more health problems
I can't stand it. I hate it. It seems this relationship has had more health problems than fun and joy. It's his fault for not fighting harder. I blame him for not fighting harder. If only there was a cure for AIDS and cancer. Why are people still suffering? It makes no sense. There is no cure. Come back to reality.

April 10th 4:20am
Just got finished watching "A Tree Grows in Brooklyn" and I think I have the answer that I've been searching for within myself. If you know the truth about a person faults and all, and know they are not perfect, it's okay to love that person and accept them for who they really are! No matter what others will say or think. No one is perfect and no matter how hard a person strives to reach perfection, nobody is perfect not even Jesus. I know that maybe that's what I was searching for in Daedalus all along. And I realize that YES I do love him and I want him in my life. I just hope that he can accept me for who I am faults and all. I think that why I've been so hard on him and myself because I know that he really truly loves me and I perhaps I didn't want him to find out that I'm not perfect. Yes I do have faults. That's what the problem has been in the midst of his illness, lately the both of us, not accepting each other for who right now and what we are and what we're about. I see now that it's going to take

time for us both to do this but it will help both of us grow and learn. Accepting someone doesn't necessarily mean you believe in their ways and ideologies, it mean respecting that person's right to voice their opinions no matter how they feel, what they think or their actions, harsh as they may be at times. Dear God thank you for helping me find my answer.

I'm asking that you give us the strength, patience, understanding to accept each other as we really are so that we may both grow in each other's love. Yes Daedalus I do love you!!! And hope that you will forever love me.

April 10th 1987-Palm Sunday 4pm
I'm at the beach and I feel at peace with myself. Dae is still in the hospital. I spoke to him this morning and it was the best conversation we've had in a long time. No arguments and no hate. I've come to realize that I do love him very much. Today is the first time I've told him in a long time. There's still so much more to come, to endure, but with the lord by my side I know we're going to make it... Thank you God for showing me the way and for giving me the patience and strength to carry on! D-

Every day I would go down to the beach and just sit and listen. The sound of the waves lulled me. I would lean back, close my eyes and lift my face up to the sky to feel the mist or sun on my face. Part of me felt as if I were flying. Part of me felt like I was falling. How can you feel two opposing movements at the same time?

Good Friday April 17th

Last night I had a dream that Daedalus died! Today is when Christ was crucified and saved the world from sin. That who so ever believeth in him shall have everlasting life. I do believe there is a God and that Jesus is the son of man and that he rose from the dead. I finally got a job working for Liz Claiborne showroom. It wouldn't have been possible without Jesus. Before I was interviewed I prayed in the name of Jesus and he made it happen.

Daedalus told me not to call him until I got a job. I haven't heard from him in 2 days. And I won't call him either. He did something that was totally uncouth. He took advantage of my offer and now I could be in a lot of trouble but lucky for me God helped me in a time of need. What he did was very foolish and irresponsible. Now he's going to borrow money from others to pay for his mistakes knowing good and well he won't pay them back. He's ruined his, his fathers and now mine. He wants the whole world to revolve around him. I don't know if we'll be together for much longer because I don't know if I want to spend my life with someone who doesn't take responsibility for his own actions. How can I have a child with him? He couldn't help me raise it because he acts like a child himself. He wants everything his way. He wants money, clothes and other nice things but he wants others to give it to him just because he wants it not need it. Instead of working and striving to get it for himself. Daedalus wants materialistic things all the time instead of trying to fulfill the void in his heart. He says stupid things like he's going to borrow $700 from Matthew to get himself and color TV & VCR. He's so intellectual but he lacks common sense.

Somewhere in the bible it says: *Answer not a fool according to his folly, lest you vow also like him. *Speak not in the ears of fools for he will despise the wisdom of thy words. Freddie Mercury from the Rock Band Queen has been diagnosed with HIV

Chapter Seventeen

Blue is the color of the red sky
Will he, will he come home tonite
Blue is the color that she feels inside
Matador, I can't hide my fear anymore
Azul es el color del rojo cielo
volvera volvera a mi esta noche
Azul es el color que siente a dentro
matador no puedo esconder mi temor-Sade
"Fear"-Sarah Mclachlan, Stuart Matthewman, Helen Adu, © Tyde Music,
Sony/ATV Songs LLC, Angel Music Ltd.

June 21st
Well, here it is June 20th or should I say June 21st cuz its 4am. I haven't written in a while. I found out Daedalus does have AIDS. I'm so scared, not for me but for him. He's getting worse and I don't know what to do. Every day I think about him dying and I can't picture him not being here, us not being together. When I look back on last summer around this time, I realized that it was such a wonderful summer, considering the things that happened... Every day I remember something or a place where we were together. When I look out on the beach from my window, I remember when we took long walks together. Last Saturday Mom & Me went to the promenade in Bklyn Heights and so many memories came back that it hurt to even think about them. Sometime it seems like only yesterday that I met him for

the first time at Bloomingdales. I couldn't stand him. He was so attractive but arrogant, cocky, obnoxious etc... The first argument we had was on the day of me being in the Miss Empire State Pageant. That Wed night he came to the house to tell me he was attracted to me. The night we went to the Garage and partied hard. The night when we first made love and spent the night in Riverside drive park. We were so happy then. I miss doing those fun things with him and out of it all the guys that I've ever dealt with, dated I can honestly and truly say that he loves me and cares about me a great deal. I realize now that I did want to have the baby but at the time he had been diagnosed with having HIV antibodies in his system. People were dying left & right, and doctors had no answers. So to be safe we both decided the best thing was to terminate the pregnancy. He was very upset because he wanted the baby as much as I did. We had so many plans individually and collectively. Now he won't have the chance to do all the things he wanted such as to get his Degree from Bard, to get a place for us, for me to take dance classes so that one day we could dance together on stage.

I thank God every day that he's alive even though he's in a lot of pain. When the phone rings I'm so frightened that it will be his Dad or sister calling me to say he died.

Recently I had a dream that I was down stairs with mom watching TV and the phone rang and mom answered saying that it was his mother Etta calling to tell me the bad news and I kept saying no, no I don't want to talk to her because I knew what she was going to say. I started screaming and yelling and crying and then I woke up. A memory flash of the village where we used to go and hangout all the time. Late at night walking, singing and having one hell of a good time. Dae and I have been through everything together. Having to deal with his past and crazy childhood. His parents letting him do some crazy shit at his age. Living with Benes, his uncle dying of AIDS, the car accident, the pregnancy, his diagnosis, deciding whether or not he should go back to school. Rareform's breakup, our breakup, not being able to find the right job, not having the things he wanted like nice clothes, his dad, his sisters, us getting back together, him getting sick again, his scar, being back in the hospital etc. I'm trying to prepare myself for the worst but you can't just plan for something like this. I can't plan for how I'll react because I have never lost someone I was intimately involved with. Sometimes I want to talk to mom and tell her everything but I know I can't so I talk to God most of the time and pray that Dae gets better or that they find a cure. I've been told that I should be tested for the HIV antibodies but I'm scared. Can I deal with the results if they come back positive? I don't want to know. Someday perhaps but not anytime soon. Things have been difficult for Dae and me and I'm trying to hold on. I'm always on the verge of tears because I love him so much. I'm trying to keep my mind busy with music, dance, work and modeling. I feel so all alone this summer. What will I do? Dae can't leave the house for long periods of time so we can't really go places. And I feel guilty about seeing other people. I know that my life has to go on but how can I have a good time when Dae is so sick? I realized the other day that I'm attracted to Ray. Oh boy what a fucking problem. I haven't heard from Sec since we did the Gospel Fest. He's back on coke again. I think its crack. I pray that GOD watches over him and helps him through the bad times. Sec, Dae and I had so much fun together and I miss that and love both of them dearly. Dae finally called me after he said he thought it would be best that we didn't talk or see each other for a while. He's so confused and depressed. He said it was because he wanted to make love but he couldn't and felt so bad. I told him sex is just a part of a relationship, it isn't everything. I told him no matter what happens, in the end I'll love him always. At least he made it to his 24th birthday. Thank you God for letting Dae and me be together even if it's for a little while. A storm is coming, it's lightening outside. 6/21/87 **D.H**.

The Boy Scouts have a motto that says, *"Always be prepared. Always be in a state of readiness in mind and body to do your duty."*

There was an angry storm rising within me. A destructive emotional storm that would inevitably come in and wash away a part of my life. And I couldn't turn my focus from it. It was in that dark part of me just beneath the surface. Percolating.

Waiting. Lurking. My sanity was trying to handle the pressure that was building. How was I supposed to prepare for a storm when never having been in one like it before?

What emergency supplies should I get in order to try and stabilize my sanity and emotions? How many candles was I supposed to buy so that I'd be able to see some light at the end of the spinning vortex? How many bottles of water would I need to stock up on to replenish the tears that I would cry? Would I have enough blankets to keep me warm when the cold reality crept in that I will lose my lover and best friend? Maybe a first aid kit. Yes, they say preparation is key if you are to survive right?

Let's see, I'll need an antiseptic to clean the wounds and scrapes to my psyche. Some antibiotic ointment for the blisters that are forming from the chafing of what my heart hopes and begs for against the conflict of what my mind knows to be true. I'll need some sterile bandages, to control the bleeding and cover the multiple injuries of what this loss will bring; so as not to contaminate the other areas of my life and the people around me. Let's, throwing in for good measure, pain-killers. Yes indeed! I'll need something, anything that will explicitly shut down the signals to my nervous system so I won't feel the pain that will soon become my life.

Queen Elizabeth II once said, "Grief is the price we pay for love."

Sunday June 21st-22nd 12:30AM
Daedalus and I went to see the movie Crocodile Dundee in Brooklyn Heights. It was okay. We went for a bite to eat afterwards. He stopped and got some flowers and fruit. I must say he looked fab in his turquoise today. We kissed a lot in the theatre. When we got outside I felt people staring at me & him. He had on house slippers due to the beginning stages of peripheral neuropathy in his feet and hands. This was one of the side effects of the "cocktails" often vital to the patient taking as many as 30 pills a day. Some had to be taken with food, others on an

empty stomach. Some had to be taken twice a day, some every eight hours.

Juggling the requirements of Dae's medications was a full- time job. And the side-effects were severe. There was his extreme sensitivity to touch, the tingling, prickling, or burning sensations. Sharp pains and cramping. He soon began experiencing loss of balance and coordination, loss of reflexes and muscle weakness. There were noticeable changes in the way he walked. He had difficulty walking up and down stairs and frequently stumbled. We were always so afraid he would fall. He had to avoid extended periods of standing or walking and this is why he had no choice but to wear house slippers at all times. His only other option was to discontinue this dangerous drug cocktail that caused the peripheral neuropathy and have his T-Cells drop.

I know he looked gaunt. Pale and very emaciated. I couldn't take it. I don't know why but for a brief second I felt embarrassed to be romantic with him out in public. I went back to his house for a while. He held me close and caressed me. It felt so good that it brought back memories from last summer. I wonder sometimes does he remember as much as I do. Every detail? I think he's going to get better. I pray that he does. We still didn't get to talk about certain things. Maybe it's for the best.

There are so many things that I want to tell him but when it comes down to conversation, I can only say "I love you. Sec called him today which did him good I think. Sec hasn't spoken to me since the Gospel Fest and I couldn't care less. While we were lying down talking, we started kissing again and at that moment I became so overwhelmed I started to cry. Dae & I haven't made love since before he gave me this journal in March. Oh how I wish we could but… I wonder what we'll do for 4th of July. I really don't care, just as long as we're together. I'm glad I'm writing again. It helps me get out a lot of the anger, fear, sadness and frustration. It got to the point where I couldn't even open this book to write knowing that Dae gave it to me. I'm hoping we can become closer to each other. Daedalus I love you. Thank you God for making this day possible.

I received a note on a sheet of yellow legal pad that simply said "Deirdre I ♥ U" Daedalus- June 23, 1987- 8:50am Just got another sweet card from Daedalus; its two moon doggies sitting on a hill looking at the moon and stars. They touch noses. It says "your nose is cold" inside it read …but I love you anyway! Dear Deirdre- You've been so good to me, so ♥ing and kind, I just want to Thank You… Daedalus-June 24th, 1987

July 11th

I hope everything goes well. After my rehearsal Dae and I are going to the movies today to see Adventures in Baby Sitting. Ricky ended up coming with us. I hope it was ok with Dae. Overall it was a beautiful day. His energy level was high, we walked around the village and went to the park. I got mom this cute baby Minnie Mouse picture.

July 12th

Dae and me went to the village and saw Hollywood Shuffle. It was okay but made a heavy statement about *actors of color trying to survive in the business. Went back to Dae's house. It was nice spending the night, us holding each other. We both talked about how important touching and caressing has become since we can no longer make love the traditional way. It's been a while. However, our relationship was always more important than sex. He was in so much pain while we were out today because his feet started to swell. The neuropathy was getting worse. He wanted to go home because he was experiencing the burning, stiffness and a loss of feeling in his toes and soles of the feet. Sometimes the nerves in his fingers, hands, and wrists were also affected. He's also dealing with dizziness. He's getting weaker.*

Gone was the sensation of looking and feeling like a movie star. My eyes were open but I did not want to see, to know. Knowing would mean accepting. Accepting would be like rust on a razor that threatens the throat; impending danger.

Tues July 14th
I'm feeling somewhat depressed. I came home, ate a sandwich and was listening to the radio when all of a sudden I wanted to break down and cry. I prayed to God to get me through this. Then Dae called me. Perhaps it was a sign from God. I felt a little better after I hung up with him. There's a mini concert on KISS FM playing Sade's entire album. How beautiful because she is one of our favorite artists. His grandmother made me feel really bad yesterday and I will never forget. His father asked me if I wanted to go to Grenada with Dae to visit his sister Keisha. I might go or I'm seriously think about it. Sade

reminds me of Dae so much, I want to cry. Dae is going to NC Saturday to visit his mom. I hope he enjoys himself. I get the feeling that he's not coming back and it scares the hell out of me!! This week and next week I should have the rest of the money for my teeth. Grandma had a slight heart attack and didn't tell anyone. I hope she doesn't die! God thanks for letting me be here today and Daedalus. Give me the patience, strength and understanding. Amen.
Got a note today from Daedalus:
Hi Baby, Don't be lonely, cause I Love You and I'm with you, thinking of U this very moment, I miss u!
Daedalus- July 15th 1987 -7:20pm

I just got the most beautiful card from Daedalus and it brought me to tears. In it was a poem by Daniel Haughian titled:

I Will Love You...
As long as I can dream,
as long as I can think,
as long as I have a memory...
I will love you.
As long as I have eyes to see
and ears to hear
and lips to speak...
I will love you.
As long as I have a heart to feel...
a soul stirring within me,
an imagination to hold you...
I will love you.
As long as there is time,
as long as there is love,

> *as long as there is you,*
> *and as long as I have a breath*
> *to speak your name…*
> *I will love you,*
> *because I love you*
> *more than anything*
> *in all the world.*
> *Thank you for standing by me… I love you*
> **Daedalus- July 17, 1987**

July 20th, 1987 12:40am
I spoke to Daedalus this evening in NC. I miss him. He mentioned that he saw "Jaws" at the movies and went to Red Lobster. I hope he enjoys himself. His mother is still recovering from a bad cold. I hope he doesn't catch it because it could be fatal for him. In the back of my mind, I see him not ever coming back. I hope it's just my imagination. I haven't smoked since Friday. With God's help and my willpower I'm going to stop completely. I will start laying down tracks for my demo tape. Hope all goes well.

August 17th 7:30am
I'm on the D train going to work. Today is the last day that the harmonic convergence is taking place all over the world. People are gathering in Central Park. It's supposed to be the coming of a new age. It's the time when the planets all align themselves and opens up a staircase or pathway for higher spiritual consciousness. If we all pray and meditate for universal peace and harmony it will have an effect on our planet. If there aren't enough people who pray it will bring destruction to the world.

Last night I was thinking to tell Dae that I couldn't go on this way. We talked and both decided that since we couldn't make love then we would continue to hold and caress each other to keep the closeness between us. However lately he doesn't hold me or caress me. He rarely kisses me. I feel so empty. It hurts so much. I'm losing him.

August 17th 9:00pm
I just got home and I feel so tired. Mom and I were trying to choose 3 pictures from my photo-shoot with Donna and Eric. I visited Daedalus this evening. Why because he wanted to see me. I got there and not a hug, not a kiss, nothing. Then came the silence. Well it was mostly me. He asked me what was wrong and like always I say nothing. Why do I lie? I'm so afraid for him. I don't want him to die. I don't want him to leave me. I haven't been feeling well. I don't want him to worry about me. He begged me to talk to him. I said "what about you and your pain?..." I didn't mean to sound so cruel and he began to cry. I felt so terrible inside. Why was I so mean to him? He took some valium to calm himself down and then dosed off. I had to lock the door behind me because he wouldn't get up. I left feeling depressed as ever, so lonely and empty again. Ashamed for hurting him. Thank you God for letting me and Dae see another day.

Chapter *Eighteen*

You are my love
You are my Heaven
You are my love
Make me sing la, di, da
You are my love
You are my Heaven Darling, I, oh
I won't let them take you away- Roberta Flack & Donny Hathaway
"You Are My Heaven", Eric Mercury, Stevie Wonder, ©Jobete Music Co. Inc.

Sunday August 23rd
I'm taking a hot bath right now trying to ease my mind. It's been a week since I last saw Dae. I hope he's doing better. I miss him so much. Maybe I'll call him tomorrow at work.
Got called into Jorge's office on Friday after getting in 20 mins late. He says if I don't straighten up I will be terminated. People have been telling him that I've been putting them on hold and forgetting about them. He's getting his messages a day late which is hard for me to believe.
I think that's why I can't see Dae because his illness is affecting my job performance. I spoke to Ray yesterday and we talked for a long time about Secotine and him possibly being gay and in the closet about it. Sec acted so strange at rehearsal Friday I hope he can overcome his problems. Ray also told me to try and prepare myself for Daedalus' death. He had a friend who just died from AIDS and it was hard on him. When the time comes I

think I would like to do something musical for Dae's funeral. Didn't We Almost Have it All by Whitney Houston? Ray asked me what I wanted to do with myself and my music career because he has something coming up that he thinks would be good for me. Hope it goes well.

September 27th
It's the beginning of the end.... The Paradise Garage has been closed....No more waking up around 9pm, having dinner, watching SNL, make-up, hair, clothes.
I'll never forget the feeling of joy as we came up from the subway at Houston Street. The elation of strutting up that ramp. There was no air-conditioning or central heating. They didn't sell alcohol, which meant we could stay and dance until noon the next day. Oh my god the sound system was like nothing I had ever heard before. Larry Levan was a GOD! Those marathon filled Saturday night sets he played always ended up taking us exhausted, sweaty disciples- black, white, straight and gay in one place to "church" Sunday mornings by playing music by gospel-voiced divas that sermonized us by way of full-length vocal verses and choruses about love, togetherness, freedom of expression. We'd come out into the blinding afternoon sunlight, go to the diner for brunch and head back to Brooklyn for a shower and much needed sleep. Just to do it all again.

Got a note from Daedalus today.
"Just a little note to say I love you, I think about you and I miss you terribly."
Daedalus-October 16, 1987

October 17th 1987

Dae called me Friday. We talked a little while. He told me he was leaving for NC the end of this month and he wouldn't be back until around Christmas. At that moment I thought, "I guess I'll be spending my birthday alone as usual. I then started to cry because he wouldn't be here with me on my birthday. I will miss him so much but most of all because I love him so much till it aches my heart.

October 19th

Today is Monday. It's now 4:15am and I can't sleep. I spent the night at Dae's last night. We went to see Anita Baker at Radio City. I didn't have to wait even 5mins because he was there on time. He bought me a beautiful white Gardenia. I didn't really have much to talk about. We haven't seen each other in about 3 weeks or more. It's funny that we are so close and yet so far apart. We have this unspoken connection. I can think about him and he'll call because he says he felt I was thinking about him and vice versa. I don't know if he realizes it but he has a special inner sight. He can talk to me without saying a word and I can feel what he feels. He is now having difficulty walking up and down stairs and frequently stumbles.

I really loved the concert. I listened to every note that Anita sang. I thank God Dae and I had another beautiful day together. When we got out of the concert I couldn't decide if I wanted to go home or to his place. I ended up at his house. He made some spaghetti which was fab, watched a little TV and then went to sleep.

In the middle of the night I felt him kiss me so sweetly twice. Early the next morning I opened my eyes and he was staring at me. Guess he was watching me sleep. He awakened me with a kiss so tender that it made my heart jump (as corny as it may sound.) I was so scared at first that I kissed him very cautiously but it only took a moment for me to return kisses back to him, this time with so much love that it overwhelmed me. I think he wanted to make love but we didn't. We laid in bed all day just holding and caressing one another. It was so beautiful that at one point I began to cry. It felt beautiful yet confusing to me. I love this beautiful human being and yet he's dying right before my eyes. We've been through so much together and it's incredible to me that we still have such strong feelings for each other. At the concert it felt as if every song that Anita sang spoke to the specialness of our relationship, the love we have for each other, shared memories. Our relationship is so complex at times. Lately there has been so many negative things going on but I love him and I know that he loves me and I hope our love will last forever. Thank you Lord for there is no one I'd rather share my love and life with than with Dae.

It's now Tuesday morning 3:00am I'm going to meet with the President of this fashion company. I hope all goes well. I had a dream that I was coughing up big clots of blood… that's all I remember.

I finally got Dae's letter today. It said "I love you, I've been thinking about you and I miss you terribly Love Daedalus"

I tried to call him today but got no answer. I wanted to tell him how much I enjoyed the weekend with him so much. I know at times I say bad things about him but most of them I don't really mean. Just when I think it's too much to handle and I talk of leaving him or giving up, I never will give up! I'm thinking about joining a health club or taking dance classes. Maybe I can talk O.T. into joining with me. Thank you god, for letting me see another day.

Wed Morning Oct 21st 2:00am
Well what-a-ya know! All went well today, I got the job. It seems kind of boring but then again it was my first day. I called Dae this morning. He told me he loved me and vice versa. I tried calling him twice today but no one answered. I called again and the line was busy. So damned frustrating. I told him to take his answering machine back from Athena. She's so selfish. He needs it more than she does. I really dislike her because of how she treats him. I try not to but I can't help it. His parents should have broken her out of her hatefulness and selfishness when she was little then maybe she wouldn't be the way she is now. I wonder if she believes in God. Thank God for giving me another chance to be among the working class again. I trusted in you when I got fired and you brought this job to me

October 25th
It's now 2:30am. I can't sleep. I spoke to Dae and he didn't sound too good. He'll be leaving next Sunday Oct 31st to stay with his mother in NC. He says he'll be back before Christmas. I feel sad because I'm going to miss him

but I think it will be good for him. I'm also afraid he won't come back. I don't know if I can handle that. I pray that he does... I'm trying to keep my spirits up for his sake as well as mine and I know if I break down and cry he will too. This all seems like a dream to me and I'm going to wake up and things will be back to normal. Dae wouldn't be sick and we'd still be hanging out together doing things that we planned to do. Why do things have to be this way? Why? Why? Why? I'm going to cease my writing because I'm starting to cry and get real emotional and I'm afraid I won't be able to stop. Daedalus I miss you already and you're not even gone yet. I love you...

I received a collection of Love poems from Dae. In the card he said: D- You are truly the ♥ of my life- I thank God we have each other! I love you as never anyone before. Daedalus- October 28, 1987

Tuesday December 8th, 1987
It's been over a month since I've gotten the urge to write. I had a fabulous birthday, I went to NC. Dae and his mom threw me a little party with Smurf party favors. He bought me a camera but wrapped the box so he could use the camera to take pictures. We were intimate with each other the first night I got there. It was so beautiful. Then we sat up and talked. I realize as each day passes that I love him more and more.

Monday I'll be performing at a cast party for the Off Broadway show "Don't Get God Started". I hope we do well. At last Fridays rehearsal some clients came by to hear what the "Lighthouse Singers" sound like because they are looking to invest some money. John and Sec are really becoming a nuisance to the group. I don't think they'll last. John is in his bag and comes off like he's doing the group a favor by singing with us. He sings the songs half-assed most of the time and acts like he couldn't give a shit whether we sound good or bad. I don't understand how in the hell he can show his face after rehearsals when he hardly shows up for them. He never comes to any of the 'minor' performance but only wants to sing for the special engagements.

Sec is so high strung or strung out. He's a ball of nervous energy. He lives in a dream world always playing a game of make believe with himself. He believes that he is such a great singer and he knows his "craft". Actually he doesn't know shit. It takes him too long to learn notes and harmonies and always sings flat. He comes to me with these outrageous stories about him singing for a commercial or TV series.

About some girl in Washington DC who wants him. He's going to miss rehearsal for our gig to fly and see her. He calls me for advice. This should be made into a TV show call "Life Styles of the infamous Light House Singers"

I tried to call Dae. There was no answer. I miss him so much. The cast party performance went well. They loved us! I said hello to Barbara our future manager and she didn't speak. There's something about this woman that I don't like. I get the feeling she doesn't like me. We performed for the 100 Black Men Coalition. We sucked! Sweetwater's was ok. They asked us to fill the Sunday brunch spot. Christmas was so good this year except Dae was in the hospital again. This time he contracted pneumonia and this was scary. Just a common cold could kill him. They thought he wouldn't make it. He had a seizure that almost killed him. After he got better another incident followed.

He went on a talking rampage… He was talking nonstop for 12 hours straight that finally they had to sedate him. After that episode, then he wouldn't take his medication, he wouldn't eat. He was dying all over again. Then he got on this religious thing. Perhaps he found God.

Deep down in my heart I truly believe Dae found God and believes there is a higher being who watches over you, protects you, comforts you and is a friend to you always. He finally made it back to NY safely for Christmas.

We didn't spend time together because I spent Christmas at Ricky's with his family and friends in Ohio. I had a wonderful time! Ricky's sister Vicky cooked like she was crazy or something. There was soooo much food. I finally gave Dae his gifts. He loved it. His mom loved her scarf. It's such a shock to me to see Dae in the state that he's in. He's lost so much weight and looks so emaciated. He was such a health nut when I met him. Juicing, brown rice, raw foods and vitamins. All he used to think about was his clothes, hair, his skin, face. He's cold all the time. Now he walks around in thick heavy socks, long johns, pajamas and 2 sweaters, a robe, winter hat and gloves. He's become so paranoid and thinks everyone has a cold and it's going to kill him. He's even resorted to wearing a surgical mask around the house. Can you blame him?

December 31st 1987

Well its New Year's Eve and I'll probably spend it alone again. Seriously thinking about going to church. Dae and I have been on the phone for 2 maybe 3 hours arguing over stupid nonsense. He doesn't want to spend New

Year's Eve with me. I know we can't do anything extravagant although I would love to. I just wanted to be with him. He finally hung up on me. I get in bed to go to sleep and an hour later he calls and says I'm right we should spend it together. We went out for Chinese food in Brooklyn Heights. We had so much fun down there last summer. Bike riding, walking around, eating at different spots. We always ended up at the promenade and just smooched on the balcony. I remember being there for the 4th of July to watch the fireworks. It was a beautiful memory. I miss all the things we did together. The Village was our home away from home. And Riverside Drive Park... I will never forget that night as long as I live. Daedalus I love you!

My journaling became disorderly and irregular. I had already started losing track of time, even days and it was getting worse. My normal state of awareness was becoming impaired. My exterior may have showed little to no sign of trouble but my mind was in a dark place I couldn't escape from. The anxiety and depression was altering my sense of identity, memory and consciousness. The brain is such an amazing, extraordinary organ. I think my mind was helping me cope by way of disconnecting from myself and life. Whereby I was disassociating from the distressing events in my consciousness, shielding me from the pain and the fear associated with the trauma that was unfolding. I was exhausted. Fatigued from the weighted feelings of guilt of anger, of feeling suicidal. My body felt broken down from the heaviness of carrying this alone. I socially withdrew and my sleep and appetite became unstable.

Chapter *Nineteen*

Oh oh, Thinking about U driving me crazy
Oh oh, My friends all say it's just a phase,
but ooh-ooh, Every day is a yellow day
I'm blinded by the daisies in your yard.-Prince
"Condition Of The Heart"- Prince Rogers Nelson ©Controversy Music

Happy New Year. 1988 is here and I'm so glad that I got to spend it with Dae.

Date?
What a weekend this has been. Tomorrow it's back to work. I just spent the entire weekend with Dae telling me what I "should" eat. Telling me things about his life that would shock the hell out of you. I listened. All I did was listen and that made him angry because he says I never talk to him anymore. When I do we just argue so I just listen. I am Dae's girlfriend, lover, friend, mother, father, sister and therapist. He wears me out sometimes. I did suggest we do some counselling together so I can understand better why this virus makes him act this way. And for him to also let go some of his fear, frustration, anxiety and anger he's keeping locked up inside of himself. His mother called and said that the doctors in NC said that he is on the verge of a nervous breakdown. The medication he's on makes him ramble, say things he

> *can't remember saying and live in a fantasy world. Dae keeps saying he's going back to Bard when he knows he can't really ever go back. We had a fabulous time upstate at Bard College. I remember the first time I went with him, we were just friends at the time. He was telling people that I was his fiancé. When we spent the night in Kelly's room, I put on his t-shirt. He kissed me. The next morning Kelly left for class and we drove back to NYC. I felt so attracted to him that I wanted him to take me right there on the floor. It didn't happen. As we packed up, he kissed me... right then and there*
> *I knew I loved him!*

Eventually Dae he had to leave school for good because his health was deteriorating so rapidly. He was brought back to NY about a week later. We talked on the phone about when he got back to school he was going be taking his ballet/ dance classes so he could be prepared for audition's and go out on tour.

Not sure when but at some point we had a terrible argument. Being the stubborn people that we were, we didn't call and talk to one another. A week passed. His mother called me and told me he was in the hospital. This would make the 5th time in the past few months. She wasn't sure if he would make it. He had another infection but this time it was on his brain and other places in his body.

As 1987 came to a close 71,176 people were diagnosed with AIDS in the US, and 41,027 are now dead.

I dropped everything at work and rushed to St. Claire's Hospital; thinking to myself, is this it? Please don't let this be it! I prayed to God to let him make it to January and he did. I always prayed so hard and he had pulled through so many times before and got better. Each time I prayed I asked for another month. I kept praying for him to make it to February and he did.

> **Saturday February 13th 1988**
> *I'm cleaning to keep my mind off of Dae being in the hospital. I can't believe he's been there since Jan 25th and no one told me! Oh yeah, his father said he called and left a message which got screwed up by dad or Chris. He now has toxoplasmosis or lesions and in HIV-infected patients is usually a complication of the late phase of the disease. Typically these lesions are found in the brain and their effects dominate the clinical diagnosis.*

The decision to treat a patient for CNS toxoplasmosis is usually based on the doctors' experience. How much experience did his doctor have? Most Health Care Practicners hadn't had lots of experience with full blown AIDS. All they knew was that the primary therapy is to be followed by long-term suppressive therapy, which is continued until the antiretroviral therapy can raise CD4+ counts above 200 cells. Prognosis is guarded. Patients relapse because of noncompliance or the increasing dose requirements.

> **Date?**
> *He doesn't have long now. They want to put a tube down his throat to feed him but his mother says no. I'm glad*

> *because I know he would hate that. He's down to about 70 pounds. He doesn't talk or move. They had to put in a catheter so he can urinate. He defecates and has to be cleaned up. He looks at me but I'm not sure he knows me. I told him I still loved him not because I feel sorry for him but because I truly honestly love him! He was the only person in my life so far that I could see myself married to. I feel so guilty, if I would have kept the baby, a part of him would live on. Athena upset me so much because as Dae lies there dying she still can't be civil to me and I know he wouldn't want that. I'm listening to tapes of us "Rareform" rehearsals. We had so much fun. All of us talented. "All is Fair in Love"*

I was so angry at his folks when I found out that he had been in the hospital since February 10th, almost a week before someone called me. But then he started to get better so it didn't matter. If I have to bargain for each month for him I would. We had wasted so much time being angry at each other. We both said hurtful things. I think it was because we were both scared of what was coming. The funny thing is; to this day I can't quite remember exactly what it was we fought about but it was something to do with me saying he wasn't fighting hard enough. By the time I got to him, he was so sick that he had lost his ability to speak. Each day I visited him. Praying for a miracle, I'd wake up and there would be a cure. I sat by his bed, held his hand in mine and told him how sorry I was that we fought and that I loved him and would always love him. And I didn't really mean it when I said that I would hate him if he didn't fight this, not to give up. The most painful thing is: I don't know if he could hear or understand me.

The nurse had inserted a catheter for him to relieve himself. He started getting purple bedsores all over his beautiful pale skin. KS they called it. He developed another infection; then the cancer arrived and eventually the diapers because he couldn't control his bowel movements any longer. It was amazing to me that his mom just took right over taking care of him. Bathing him and cleaning him. God, I thought what must have been going through her head? Here lies her only son, 25 years old slipping away. She had taken care of him when he was born and she is taking such care of him as he lay there dying. What courage!

On the last night I visited him, I finally whispered to him that it was ok for him to go and that I wouldn't hate him. That I would miss him terribly but I'd be okay. I whispered I love you with all my heart. His whole family was there. Sec was there with O.T. His sister April had made a tape of all his favorites' songs. Whitney Houston, Stevie Wonder, Denise Williams, and a song he performed in a show. We stood in a circle around his bed, holding hands, and with the music playing softly in the back ground telling him if he was ready, that it was okay for him to go. We sang to him. We stood in his presence and sent him our prayers of love and positive energy to take with him on his journey. We kept repeating to him in a quiet mellow chant, I love you. I love you. I love you. I love you. I love you. I love you.

I leaned down and whispered softly the longing of my heart song into his ear, things that I needed to say and things I know he needed to hear. I told him that I loved him so very much one final time as I looked into that beautiful face. And it was as if God had bestowed upon me another moment of grace; he finally opened his eyes which had be closed for the past few days, and Daedalus looked directly at me. I don't know if he was forgiving me. I don't know if he was saying he loved me. All I know for sure is that Daedalus looked directly at me. I could tell that he could hear and understand every word I was saying to him. His breathing was labored. I leaned in and whispered to him; Dae if you want to go, go on, it's okay. Go ahead, move toward the light. I'll be okay. Other family member moved closer to him to talk to him. I looked over at the clock. Visiting hours would be over soon. When I looked back at him, his eyes were closed again. I told him I'd be back the next day to spend the entire day with him because after all it would be February 14th, Valentine's Day and he was still my sweetheart. I gave him this large stuffed animal that I bought at the Hallmark store. It was this cute little dog with big eyes like his holding a heart in its mouth which said I love you. I told him he was the one that I loved and was still in love with. I tried to strategically place it by his bedside so if perchance he opened his eyes again he could see with no effort at all. It would be in his line of sight.

Weary and worn, I took that long train ride to Coney Island. Finally I got home but couldn't eat. I undressed and replayed the moment he looked at me over and over in my mind. It was after 1:00am. I said a prayer, got in bed and finally dozed off. About an hour later the phone rang out in the dark quite house. It was his dad. He said he's gone. He told me to take a cab back into the city, he would pay the fare. I went back to my room and screamed at the top of my lungs. I started to cry uncontrollably. I laid down on my bed and put my face in the pillow and wept. I kept asking God why. Why did you have to let him die? Why did you take him away from me? There was so much we had to do together. If there is a God why does he let people die? After about 15-20 minutes of me blaming god and bawling, my mother came up stairs a picked me up from my bed and hugged me while I cried. He's gone, he's gone.

It took me another hour to get back to him. Derryck was waiting outside to pay the cab fare. I couldn't get upstairs fast enough. Where was the elevator? What floor was he on again? I was frantic and had to get to him. Hurry up elevator! My legs were feeling like lead, numbness was setting in. I felt like I was outside my body watching this moment happen from a distant place. Finally, I got upstairs. Everyone was in the hall by his room. His mother, dad, one sister and myself. We all went in the room one last time. Oh my god. He looked so ethereal and peaceful, radiating light. Could someone really look this beautiful in death? Yes, he looked like an angel. We prayed together with the minister and everyone began saying their goodbyes.

I was the last one in the room. I told him that he was okay now. There was no more pain. I kissed his lips and said I'd always love him; that we'd meet again. I asked him to send me a sign to let me know he was all right. This is just goodbye for now.

I stayed at his house that night. His sister April and I talked and cried. I cried and shared with her the guilt that I was carrying ever since Dae got sick. Maybe I should have kept the baby. Now that he's gone there would still be piece of him here. She told me not to think like that. She said you can't play what ifs. She asked what if I did carry to term and the baby died from the virus, could I live with myself? Part of me knew she was right but at that moment I wanted what I wanted. Him or a piece of him in the flesh.

I called Sec and Ray and told them he was gone. We all grieved together. I'm so grateful that they let me be there with him until the very end and share in their sorrow. Their grief of losing their beloved son, brother and grandson.

I remembered his grandmother who lived downstairs, coming upstairs to his room. It was a hot summer's day so I was lying down across the bed with just my slip and camisole on. She must have thought something was going on because he was also lying down with just his t-shirt on. Little did she know that at that time we were just friends trying to stay cool in the summer heat. In her Caribbean dialect she said "I don't know you're doing but I don't want any BLACK grandbabies!"

His family was black but she didn't consider them to be because of their light complexion and being a well to do family from the Caribbean islands. I was shocked. This was probably one of the first times my color had been an issue to another black person. He defended me; they argued and didn't speak to each other for a while.

Chapter *Twenty*

Let the dishes wait, no need in dusting
No reason to clean the dirty floor
'Cause I'm sure it doesn't matter
Now that he has gone away
I've got no plan for the future 'cause he's not here today

Let them go to the park and I'll sit alone here in the dark
No joy left in my heart anymore.
Let me hold on to my memories,
And if I die this way just let it be
I have no plan for the future 'cause he's not here with me

Why should I comb my hair
When I know, I'm not going anywhere?
Why should I keep right on giving,
When I've lost my only reason for living?
So go on, just go on and have yourself a ball
I have no plan for the future 'cause he's not here
I have no plans for the future 'cause he's not here at all-Natalie Cole
"No Plans For The Future" Marvin Yancy; Jr. Jackson, ©Chappell & Co.

Wednesday February 17th 12:40am
Well, he's gone. This is the first thing that pops into my head when I open my eyes from my restless sleep. Dae finally passed away. He died in the early hours on Valentine's Day morning. What an auspicious day to leave this world don't you think? I hope he was at peace. I don't think I can go on without him in my life. I knew it was going to happen but why now? I wasn't ready... God how come you haven't made it possible for people to

> *find a cure for AIDS? Why, why why? I miss you so much. There are things I know I should have told you. I just hope you knew through all of our bad times I loved you. Everywhere I go there's something to remind me of you. Every minute, I wish I could die so that we can be together forever. I will never fall in love with anyone for the rest of my life.*

How do you describe the moment of being in a strange limbo where the reality of your life becomes slow motion and everything around you becomes unimportant and falls away?

As soon as I am awake and am aware of myself and surroundings, I can't catch my breath. Instantly, I forget how to breathe. I remember all the vivid surrealistic details of that morning. The morning of his funeral. How the molecules of grief danced in the air. How my fingers felt clumsy and heavy as I tried to apply a bit of makeup to my swollen, ashen face. I kept starring at my face in the mirror. It was me but not me. Fragments of noise from the apartment above were intruding on my thoughts. There was a stirring of people outside in the cold. Going about their business not knowing that I had just lost my love. My limbs were numb. I felt each drop of the fear and apprehensiveness of being in the world without him. The pit of my stomach was on fire. I wanted him here with me. To hold me softly, never letting me go. To smell his damp hair after a shower, to hear his heart beating. Sitting on the edge of my bed starring out the window I melted into soft tears. The loneliness. Hollow.

His service was held at Redden's Funeral home on 14th street in Chelsea. Lots of people were there. We all looked the same as we did last week and the weeks before but now we all moved like robots. Mechanical in the way we were walking, talking, sitting, and standing. Sounds of my surroundings were muffled as if everyone was trying to hold a conversation under water. It seemed as if the world, my world had decelerated to a sluggish tempo. I wondered if this slow-motion effect was my brain's way of trying to making sense of it all.

Date?

Daedalus. Daedalus it's so hard to just write your name. I try to whisper your name in hopes that you hear me, feel me, that it softens the blow but your beautiful name gets stuck somewhere in between my heart and mouth. You were so energetic, witty and at the same time gentle and loving. Besides my mother you were my best friend. I wish I could have met you earlier in my life. You gave me love, joy, peace. You believed in me, my music, you stuck by me when the chips were down. We became lovers, which brought us closer maybe too close. It hurts so much. You were gentle, tender, warm, soft, caring, loving, funny, and dramatic, daring. Dae you were so beautiful to me. Even though we fought a lot, the sicker you became the more beautiful the essence of you became. Yes there were times when I was with you and thinking how I was slowly and painfully losing you, yes panic did sweep over me most of the times that I felt like running out of your apartment. I never feared you. I feared for your life but was never afraid or repulsed. I was never really going to abandon you while you were sick. I didn't think twice about just lying down and napping with you. Thoughts did run through my mind that I could be sick myself. We were almost parents. We were almost husband and wife. We were going to travel to Italy, Jamaica, Paris, and Boston. We were going to move in together. We were going to sing together. Just you and I. You were going to teach me to swim, how to ride horses, how to drive. You were showing me how to enjoy life. Then came the car accident, the pregnancy, HIV diagnosis, the abortion, AIDS, your death on Valentine's Day!!!!

Didn't we almost have it all?
When love was all we had worth giving
The ride with you was worth the fall my friend
Loving you made life worth living…..Whitney Houston

Date?
Why does it hurt so much? I think I'm going crazy! Tears. Daedalus where are you? Why did you have to die and leave me all alone? I feel like killing myself. Maybe I will. When you died a part of me died with you.

Date?
Daedalus I see you seeing me. We'll be together soon.

Date?
What if I have AIDS too? Am I going to die just like Dae did or worse? No one knows, no one cares. Fuck everybody

Date?

My head hurts. Dae would say I don't drink enough water. Maybe I have a brain tumor and my heads about to explode all over the room. Mom will have to clean it up piece by piece, drop by drop. Ha Ha Ha Ha

Date?
Maybe sleep will bring me death. I bet mom and dad never loved each other as much as Dae and I did. I should have kept the baby. Maybe because we didn't talk to each other since New Year's weekend he just gave up. I killed him. I killed Daedalus.

Memories. Laughter. Celebrations. Conversations. Quarrels. Last words. These seven words, rotating. Memories. Laughter. Celebrations. Conversations. Quarrels. Last words. Like a Rubik's cube, turning them over and over and over in my mind. I felt like I was dying. In fact I longed for death to take me away from what was to come. What I had to face; my future, myself, my life, my choices.

Date?
At the house, that big old white house. We had so much fun. We made love in the kitchen and got caught. We were as close as anyone. We talked & talked. Derryk came to visit, the poetry reading..... I'm not afraid to die.

Date?
Love, Sex, Lust. There's not a day that goes by when I don't think about you. I still sometimes cry. Missing you soooo much.... I feel like everybody wants something

from me. Why? Mom, dad, Ricky, Ray, Tasha, Wanda, Secotine, O.T. Why why why?
Am I pretty enough, smart enough, strong enough… Why?
There will never be another love like yours and mine. Daedalus I miss you, I love you, Deirdre.

Date?
What am I going to do with myself? I'm so angry, confused and hurt. Music makes me cry. Sec I hate you, OT I hate you, Barbara I hate you, Ray I hate you. Daedalus I love you. Deirdre

Without will or consciousness is how I moved through the new normal of my days. The loss of Dae felt like a cold gray tombstone, thick and unmoving. I welcomed the bitter cold and winds of winter. I wished for it to snow so heavily that I would be locked inside of this house forever.

March 1988
Had a dream. I went to the bank to take out money with my cash card, it was so crowed. I saw people that I knew but I can't remember their names. A riot broke out. I got shot. Next thing I knew I was laying outside on the sidewalk. Policemen were everywhere holding rifles, guns and they were telling me to stay down out of the way not knowing that I was already shot. The bank robbers were on one side of the street, the police on the other. I tried so hard to get up and run but my feet were like lead. I got shot again. It was wonderful because I felt no pain. Next thing I knew I was floating up and up and

up. I wasn't scared because I knew I would soon be with Daedalus. I was floating so high up I could see every building, every car, every block. It was such a beautiful day. It was sunny and the sky was blue, not one cloud existed. It felt about 80 degrees. All I could do was smile because I was so happy.

May 1988

Tomorrow is the AIDS walk-a- thon. In a way I want to be there. Dae birthday is coming soon. I still miss him. It hurts just thinking about him. I started collecting the materials I'll need for is quilt so it will be ready by June. Why do I feel so alone? I tried calling Etta for Mother's Day but her phone was busy and then later on no one was home. Well another one of us is gone. Joe Williams died of AIDS. We sang at his funeral and it was like Dae dying all over again. I couldn't take it.

I'm going to go and get tested. Maybe I'll feel better knowing the results and that I'll be with Dae again but in another lifetime? What if I test positive? I'm so scared and I feel so depressed, like I can't go on anymore. All I do every night is cry myself to sleep. Why, why why?

…You took me riding in your rocket and gave me a star
And about a half a mile from heaven
You dropped back down to this cold, cold world… (Steve Wonder)

All alone. God help me. I don't know what to do anymore and its hurting too much. All I do is hurt. Some days a little less some days a lot more but it still hurts. If I do have AIDS I wouldn't blame Daedalus. In a way I would be relieved. He kept at me to get tested. He was devastated

that he might have infected me and I know it weighed heavily on his mind. But I couldn't add to his burden.
Didn't we almost have it all?
When love was all we had worth giving
The ride with you was worth the fall my friend Loving you makes life worth living.
Didn't we almost have it all?
The nights we held on till the morning You know you'll never love that way again
Dae, didn't we almost have it all... ... (Whitney Houston)

May 16th 1:00am
Hi Dae-
I miss you. I love you. Just sitting here in the dark thinking about you as always. I finally made an appointment for this coming Sat at 2pm. To get tested for the virus. No one knows. I'm scared. Maybe I'll cancel. I'll probably go through with it. I'm smoking a cigarette. I know how you hated it when I smoked. I've been doing a lot of that lately. I'm sorry. I feel like getting stoned out of my mind right now. Remember when me you and Sec used to smoke some weed together? That was one of those keepsake memories.
How come you weren't more careful about who you slept with? I wonder who the person is that gave you the virus and if he's still alive? How many others will suffer from his stupidity? What about the person who gave it to him. Could it be Matthew who gave it to you? Someone that I've met before. You told me everything about you and you knew there were 3 people who could have given it to

you but you never told. It doesn't matter now, because you're gone.

May 22, 1988
Daedalus would be 25 years old today.

May 31st
I'm so angry at Derrick & Etta. How could they not tell me Dae was in the hospital?? I feel so bad because the last time we spoke to each other we had a fight. I never got to say I was sorry and now it's too late. I never got to make my peace with him when he was still lucid and could speak. Maybe he thought that I didn't care anymore and he got worse. We were both so stubborn. No one was going to say sorry first. It's too late, too late, too late. What am I going to do this summer without you?
You took me riding in your rocket and gave me a star
And about a half a mile from heaven You dropped back to this cold, cold world... (Steve Wonder)
No friends. No friends at all. They just don't understand. Never will. Never will. I can't help it. I love you. Went to the Village yesterday. It hurt so much. I just knew I'd run into you. I'd see your face. Will I ever again?

May 30th
Today is Memorial Day. We would have had so much fun. But never again.
...Never, Never, Never- Never run away...-Heart

Date?
This is Gay Pride week, I'm going to Central Park to see the quilt. I haven't even begun to put Dae's together yet. The parade on Sunday was wild as usual. 1 year ago since

the car accident. I miss your early morning phone calls. I'm going to buy a crystal-I hope it helps.

June 29th
Had a dream. Was in the old neighborhood on Jefferson Avenue and I ran into Annette. (My cousin who I haven't spoken to in years and didn't know Dae) She told me they buried Daedalus a couple of days after the Memorial service. I started crying and got really angry because no one told me. I went to Daedalus house and it was all boarded up and for sale. Where did they go? Then I'm in someone's house with Ray and another person. Ray kisses me and tells me not to cry. He tells me how I should kiss him. All of a sudden he has these tiny white food particles in his mouth, I then have them in my mouth too. I spit them out... I wake up. I feel so all alone. There is a full moon tonight. I cry. I hurt. I try to sleep but cant. Around this time last year Dae was still traumatized by the car accident and couldn't walk. We went to the Promenade in Brooklyn heights to watch the fireworks. I miss you. I love you. If only I could have you back. If only I could be with you. Maybe sooner than anyone expects...

Date?
I'm going to see a Channeler. Maybe he can help answer some questions for me. Maybe he can contact you or you can speak to me through him. I do believe in God and Jesus Christ his son. Ray and Leon didn't want me to go to their performance out here in Brighton Beach. That's okay. They'll know how it feels one day to feel sad and lonely. I want to go to the house. His house on Lincoln Place. But I can't seem to get up the courage. I miss you.

Holding me, hugging me, telling me everything would be okay...AIDS- will it ever be over? How many must perish? How many must suffer. How many must die alone. I'm glad I was with you until the end- It took me just about all my life to find someone like you. We had just begun to live. Only 2 short years together. Why did I think it would last forever knowing what I knew? Denial maybe? Hope? I haven't had a hug since you've been gone.

Date?
Ray/Leon
Wanda/Derrick
John/Mark
Sec/ Debbie
Jane/ David
Mom/Dad
Tahitia/Chris

Me- all by myself....Who will be there for me? Who will take care of me once the virus begins to ravish my body?

Chapter *Twenty-One*

When the summer came
You were not around
Now the summer's gone and love cannot be found
Where were you when I needed you last winter, my love?-Stevie Wonder
Kenneth B Edmonds, / Antonio Reid, / Daryl Simmons, © Sony/ATV Music Publishing LLC, Warner/Chappell Music, Inc.

> *July 2nd 1988*
> People. So many different people. All shapes, sizes, colors.... I'm sitting in Washington Square Park. Will I ever find someone for me? I guess I'm looking for someone like you Daedalus.
> ...Sign your name across my heart... (Terrance Trent Darby)
> I can see the playground across from where I'm sitting. Where we made out on the grass near there... Why do I feel so much better when I'm down here?
> Why did you have to go? Was it because you weren't strong enough. Could I be and not know it? I never thought about it until I met you. Have you come back? As what? As whom? Are you sitting across from me? The squirrel on the grass? Maybe you're watching me from a distance?

Date?
I finally got to do my show. When I first met you and Sec that's all I could talk about. It was at Broadway Baby. When you gave me that tiny apple from the orchard upstate at white house, I made you a promise that I wouldn't throw it away until my show. It was for you. The songs I sang were for you. Well my show is over and it's still on my dresser. I can't throw it away. Not yet. It's a part of you. It's something that keeps me bonded to you. As simple as it was, it was just another gift to say how much you loved me.

Daedalus I miss you. I haven't been out dancing since you and I hung out together at the Danceteria and the Garage. They closed the Garage. Aren't you pissed? So am I. Well I made it through this summer, barely, without you… I didn't think I would.

Oh what a surprise, your mom, dad and grandmother and Barbara came to my show. I was happy to see them and shocked that your grandmother came but then it all came flooding back. Loosing you. You not being in my life, the pain of not saying I'm sorry, of being angry with them.

I went to see Whitney Houston Aug 27th with Ray & Leon. I was there but not really there. I kept thinking about you. They spoiled my night. They had an argument in the street. We went out to dinner at the Museum Café (one of your favorite places) after the show. They left me in the restaurant all alone. I told them that they were both lucky to have each other. Don't take each other for granted because it might be too late to say you're sorry. If I could only get a hug from you… I want to start on your quilt but I'm not quite sure what I want to do, what I want to say. It has to be something you would like too. One day soon?

Songs that remind me of you/us:
Sade All (3) albums–I wonder what it was about Sade that we loved so much?
"War of the Heart"- The big white house we stayed in when you were at school and we started getting on each other's nerves.
"Is It a Crime"- You picked me up from my house for our drive upstate to Bard to visit friends at your school. You pointed out how beautiful the wind chimes were at that particular spot in the song. "Sweetest Taboo"- You telling me you were gay. Me being straight. Both of us ending up loving each other knowing people wouldn't understand.
"Sweet as Cherry Pie"- you sang this to me ALL the time.
"Blue and Jezebel"- When you tried to commit suicide with the vodka and pills at 2:00 am and I talked you into coming to my house and you spent the night and made it to the next morning.
Stevie Wonder-
"You Will Know" We sang that to you the night before you died in the hospital.
"With Each Beat of My Heart"- reminds me when I'd spend the night at your house and we'd have breakfast together.
"All is Fair in Love"- Me, you and Sec sang when we were together as Rareform. The first song that I sang really well that hypnotized you.

That's when you said you fell in love with my voice.
"Cold, Cold World"- The way I felt after you died.
Whitney Houston: "Greatest Love of All"-The first song Ray taught us as Rareform. The harmonies were beautiful when we got it right. The love that we all had for each other as friends.
"Didn't We Almost Have It All"- Our favorite song for each other. When it was all over, looking back on everything, the love we had for each other, the respect, the trust, the fun, the creativity, the laughter, the joy, the baby, the proposal, the support, the dreams, the hopes for the rest of our lives together- Didn't we almost have it all?
Madonna- "Papa Don't Preach"- After terminating the pregnancy, you kept singing this song over and over and over. You said you couldn't help it. I thought that was the most unkind, mean thing you ever did to me. You were so cruel.
Patti Labelle & Michael McDonald -"On My Own"- the first time I went to NC to meet your mother right after we terminated the pregnancy. She took good care nursing me back to health. You kept singing the wrong lyrics which DROVE ME CRAZY so I wrote them out for you and we sang it together.
Melissa Morgan-"Do Me Baby"-After we spent the night in the park. We went back to your house took a shower, made love listening to this song when Athena walks in on us.
Michael Jackson, "Human Nature"-We danced at the Garage all night into the morning. Went out on the roof. It was chilly out and I had no jacket. You had yours on and you let me put my arms around you inside your

jacket to keep me warm. You said don't get the wrong idea…

Date?
Dae, Secotine has changed or maybe I have. We're not as close as we used to be. I thought we would be closer now that you're gone but I think I've pushed him away… You knew him better than I did. I'm worried about him. He wants "it" the fame and accolades so much that it scares me. I finally bought a car. It's a red mercury lynx-stick. I bought it from John from the Lighthouse Singers. Had to call my dad to come get me because I couldn't drive it home. You would love it. I should have gotten it sooner so I could drive us around or visit you when you were sick. Everyone wants to know if I'm okay. They're worried about me. Why? Why pretend they care now that I act differently towards them, when all along they couldn't give a damn one way or another if I'm ok. People.

Mom got a puppy for me because I've been so depressed. You would have liked her. Her name is Bailey and she's so funny. I know she'd never hurt me or leave me. She gives me her love and I give her mine.

October 5th 1988
Dream- We were in Central Park. Me, mom, you, my brother and Bailey. There was a little girl and she was in this glass boat and it started moving out into the water. Bailey went into the water for a swim. I kept yelling Bailey come back, come back. She went out further and then disappeared. Mom and I went in to save her. And so did Dae and another man. They went underneath the

water but couldn't see because the water was very murky and dark, then they too disappeared. I started to cry and called out to mom but no answer. Some people appeared and began to help search. Somehow they move away all the water to one side kind of like the 10 commandments movie).

There was all of this sludge and there was Bailey, Dae and the other guy. They were stuck and couldn't move. It was gooey, slimy and smelly. Mom and I started pulling them out. Next thing I knew I was covered like water in Molasses. It was in my mouth, on my tongue.

Then I was heavily covered in this grey sludge. I was trying to talk but couldn't because it was in my mouth along with dead fish, garbage and sewage. Maybe this is why I buy my water and don't drink it from faucets...

Saturday Oct 8th

I watched News Line last night regarding the NAMES Project. The quilt is now in Washington DC and will be displayed today and tomorrow. I wanted to see it when it was at the Pier and Central Park but mom was with me that day in the Village and I changed my mind. I dreamed about Daedalus last night. I finally saw his face clearly. His beautiful eyes, his smile, his sense of humor. He was in the hospital and had grown a beard and it looked great. For some reason I was still living at 746 Jefferson in Bed-Stuy but dad wasn't there. We kissed and kissed and hugged a lot. I asked Dae did he believe we live on forever after we die. He said we do come back in another life but we don't live forever. His father and mother weren't in the dream. He told me from now on "no more sex" it was too risky. The strange thing about this dream, he seemed so peaceful and calm and more like himself. It didn't seem to bother him that he was dying. There were no tears on his part. We were all playing some game when I looked over at him and the beard was gone, his face was glowing, his eyes were bright, wide and far away. Then he died.

Daedalus, I miss you. You were my best friend. It's so hard to believe that I'll never see you again (maybe). I'll never get an "I love you" phone call at 2 or 3am in the morning. I'll never hear you sing, see you dance, recite Shakespeare. You'll never make fun of me. We'll never take walks together. We'll never hold and cuddle each other. We'll never have those crazy arguments anymore. We'll never look for apartments together. We'll never get married like we planned. We'll never make passionate love to each other. I'll never feel your lips touch mine. I'll never again get to run my fingers through your soft curly hair and hold you.

One day I will get around to your quilt. I guess I'm angry and scared because I know when I finish it I'll have to let go of you. And I can't or just don't want to. It still hurts so much. I wish I were with you sometimes. I just can't stop loving you (MJ). I can never get involved with anyone until I'm tested. I'm afraid. At least I'm dreaming about you. Before I couldn't picture your face. Till Eternity D-

Date?
I wonder how Benes is doing. Is he as hurt as I am?

October 17th-
I forgot Chris' birthday. I've been reading old letters that I sent to Daedalus. All I do is think about him. Maybe

I'm going crazy, slowly having a nervous breakdown. I'm going to call Denise at the Center. I need therapy, help. She'll probably try to talk me into getting tested. Deep down inside I know I have the virus, it just isn't making itself known yet. I'm trying to be positive, maybe God will make it where I didn't get it at all even though I was at risk. The virus can be passed on from person to person through semen and blood. I was pregnant with Dae's child. It only takes one time. Or maybe when I went to Kenneth, Keith, Eric, Kevin – damn I can't even remember his name but now that I look back he could've had the virus when I went to his apt on 76th street. In his kitchen were so many bottles of medicine and vitamins. I had my period so we didn't do anything that way…

When I die I hope all the people I ever knew remember me.

And I hope that they feel guilty and hurt as much as I do now. But you know what, then it would be too late to say you're sorry. Too late to say sorry for not really listening to you at times, sorry for not giving you a hug when you needed it, sorry for not being there when I hurt so bad that I would cry myself to sleep, sorry for taking from me emotionally and materialistically and NEVER giving. Sorry for never saying I love you.

Date?

People think that I'm so funny, crazy, exciting and always joking around. What they don't know is that I go through every day like a zombie in a daze, pretending that everything is ok. Laughing to keep from crying. Faking a smile when the tears are just behind my eyes, on the brink of spilling, running down my face. Will they really tell others what I died from or will it be a lie. A lie that I've told some people about Dae. Not because I'm ashamed but because they wouldn't understand. I hope their honesty......

People don't have to know how I got it, just what it was that I got. There was a program on the NAMES Project: people who had died of AIDS. Will they remember my name? I want a quilt made for myself. Maybe I should make Dae's and mine. Last year around this time I couldn't wait until Nov 24th to go and visit Dae in NC. I was so anxious. It was the best birthday I ever had. I wonder what I'll be doing this year.

Date?
First the sore throat, swollen glands, fevers of 102- 105. Headaches, chronic diarrhea. Unable to eat, weight loss, infections. Maybe pneumonia, blindness, sarcoma etc.... Death!

Date?
I have to get right with God. Our relationship hasn't been the same since he took Dae. I guess I blame God. I honestly believed that if I prayed and kept the faith he would spare Dae but he didn't. Why? Is this punishment for Dae being gay? Why? Daedalus wherever you are please don't wait for me!

Oct 18th 1988 12:28am
I Deirdre Louise Hall being of sound mind and body leave my last will and testimony. In the occurrence of my death my first wish is to be cremated and kept with my mother until her death. I hereby leave all my clothes if she wants

them to Wanda's daughter Iwana Kornegay. I leave my car to my only sibling, my brother Charles Christopher Hall. I leave to my mother all monies, television, VCR, camera, pictures etc. To Dad I leave you this: I really did love you in my own way even if you never loved me. If you did you never told me. Bailey- you were always the child that I never had. You were always there for me. You were brought into our family because I was so depressed. You always gave me your love and never hurt me. I know you understand more than people think you do. Here's a hug- I love you Bail's.

November 24th 2:15am

Well it's Thanksgiving Day and my Birthday. I'm feeling sad, angry, lonely, in pain and thankful. Thankful that I got to see another Birthday but as usual I'm spending it alone. Last year I was in NC with Dae. Having a birthday party with just me him and his mom. We had lots of fun, it made me feel close to him and his mother. I'm lonely because- I am. I guess I still have to learn to stand on my own two feet. Angry because you took me riding in your rocket (rocket of life) and just about a half a mile from heaven you dropped me back down to this cold, cold world. (You left me here all alone) you're dead. Pain because I know I'll never see you again. I'll never pick up the phone at 3 or 4am and you're there telling me you love me. I'll never feel your arms around me. I'll never feel your lips gently touch mine. I'll never have the baby we always wanted. I'll never meet you for dinner, a play or concert, walk in the park, watch the sun rise, and cook for each other. I'll never forget you...

I know that Dae wouldn't want me sitting home feeling sorry for myself or being depressed and missing him terribly but I feel like I'm betraying him or that I'll forget him if I'm having too much of a good time. I never got to tell you I was sorry. How could they keep you being in the hospital and near death from me? The last words we spoke to each other were hurtful words, hateful and spiteful. Can you or will you ever forgive me. Dae your last couple of days here on earth, at the hospital I was telling you that I loved you so very much. Were you able to understand me? I'll never know. I feel so fucking guilty. Did you leave because you thought I really didn't care anymore so you gave up fighting? Sometimes I want to know if I have the virus so it would put things into perspective. I would finally know the inevitable. I just want to be with you any way I can...

Ricky invited me over for Thanksgiving dinner. I don't think I'll go. I just want to get a bottle of wine or liquor, take the codeine pills I have and never wake up again.

Your mom sent me a birthday card. She doesn't know how special she is to me. I miss her, them so much. Sometimes I just want to be with them all, all the time. Subconsciously maybe I'll be closer to you. Well I'm officially 23 years old...

Happy Birthday Girl for what it's worth. When will it ever cease? I can't go on like this. It hurts too much. Dae I miss you, I want you, I can't have you, I love you. D-Sometimes I can't see your face at all. Sometimes all I dream about is you making love to me. Sometimes I see your face so clearly it scares me. The way your hair was. The peaceful look on you face after it was all over. Were

you scared? Your big beautiful eyes, sculpted cheekbones Michael Jackson would die for. Your last gasp for air.
…You are my first breath, my first smile and my morning cup of tea.
Yours is the love that I prayed for before I go to sleep and from the time I saw your face, I knew no other could erase My loving you with each beat of my heart… (Stevie Wonder)
I know no other way but to express what I'm feeling emotionally except musically. Verbally no one would understand. They never do. I'm going to call Etta. I miss her. Hope she's doing okay. I hope I don't fall apart on the phone. God give me the strength…
It's now 3:00 am 11/25-
Channel 13 has a show on the DAEDALUS Airplane that uses physical manpower only. Does this mean something or is it just a coincidence. What a fucking joke! Dear God- would you forgive me, have mercy on my soul if I took my life. Of course you wouldn't. That's the biggest sin a person can commit right? I don't know what to do anymore and I so scared that it's going to come to this. How come I bullshit so much with things I have to do or things that could help me? Sabotage? Survivor's guilt?

November 31st 7:00am
I REALLY dreamed last night! What does it all mean? Am I getting better, healing?
Dream: I woke up to go to the bathroom. The door to my room was open. I called for Bailey, thought she was in the hall. Uncle Hardy appeared. I asked for a hug. He asked if I had morning breath, I said yes. He didn't hug me.

Mom and Dad were dressed. It was raining. There were leaks everywhere in the house. They were moving the washing machine and packing boxes- to go where? I started to cry. Talked to Chris, looked out the window, and smoked a cigarette.
Then I was with Wanda on our old block in Bed-Stuy. Our concert was the same day as St. Luke's anniversary. I wanted to sing a different song. She said sing a song that Ricky sang.
I'm in a restaurant now. Beautiful, dimly lit. I see Lisa with a friend. She's eating a salad. She's nervous. She's moving away. She's waiting for her brother Tim and Ms. Grantham. Ms. Grantham walks in. Robert appears. We're happy together. He wants to take me to bed.

I got on stage in the restaurant to sing. Tim appears, we're all laughing, joking, at ease with one another. Ms. Grantham is crying, she doesn't want Lisa to move away. I think she's going away to attend college. Someplace sunny with clear skies, lots of land, green trees, serene.
I'm now in a living room with April. She's pregnant. Robert is with me. Athena comes in with her niece and says hello. She speaks to me, why? She rubs April's stomach. She asks if there's any rice. I'm lying down on the couch, staring at a wall filled with post cards I had received from Daedalus when he was alive. They were taped on the wall so you couldn't see the writing on the back. I want to read them. I'm wondering how his family is dealing with his death? Robert appears again, still wants to have sex, and changes his mind. I wake up. It all seemed so real. I read the bible last night, marked off passages. The world is coming to an end. We're living in

the last days. What does this all mean? Is Dae communicating with me? Saying it's alright? Things will get better? Was God telling me something? Will they? Will things get better? What does it all mean? What? Daedalus I still love you! D-

    Dae, Sylvester passed away. He died from complications from AIDS on December 16th. Damn it! Remember how we partied at the clubs to "You Make Me Feel, Do ya Wanna Funk & Dance. Here we are at the end of 1988 and another 106,994 are diagnosed with AIDS in the US, another 62,101 have died.

Chapter *Twenty-Two*

*Haunt me
In my dreams
If you please
Your breath is with me now and always
It's like a breeze-Sade*
"Haunt Me", Stuart Matthewman, Helen Adu, ©: Angel Music Ltd.

February 6th 1989
It's been a while since I've written. I feel scared and frightened and alone; of what I don't know. It's almost Dae's one year anniversary since he's been gone. I can't believe it's been a year. It seems like only yesterday he was here. I'm crying. It still hurts so much. Why is there still pain? I thought I was feeling better. I've been putting off keeping in contact with Etta, April, Derrick and Barbara. She called to wish me a Happy New Year. She's in town. ...It hurts...
Letter to Etta first Draft: Dear Etta-
First I want to say Happy New Year. I got your Xmas card. Thanks. I know I haven't been keeping in touch with you. Please forgive me. It all hurts still and being that Daedalus is part of you, I just can't handle seeing you or talk to you. I want to go back to the house to see Derrick but I'm not ready. Everywhere I go, be it the village, uptown, Brooklyn Heights, I'm reminded of him. Sometimes I miss Daedalus so much that I hope I get sick

and die so I can be with him. I know it sounds crazy but that's just the way I feel.

I called to make an appointment to get tested anonymously but I never went. At times I really want to know so if I'm positive then I can start preparing myself for what's to come. I've been doing ok as far as eating. I went to the doctor because I was feeling badly. He told me I was anemic and gave me some vitamins. I've been having small fevers, headaches and sleeping a lot. At times I feel like killing myself because I want to be with Dae so badly. The pain hasn't stopped for me. I doubt if it ever will but I'm trying. Anytime of the day I just think about him and cry. I know he wouldn't have wanted me to be this way but I can't help it. I didn't know you could love someone just as much in death as in life. My life would have been great; I think we would have finally gotten our apartment. We would have a daughter. He would still be in college; I would be performing and working on my music. I quit my job to pursue my music and acting full time. It's a little rough right now but it'll get better. I hope that if its Gods will, and I do have AIDS I hope there will be someone to take care of me.

Saturday-February 11th 1989 5:35am

I finally wrote the letters to Etta & Derrick. It was hard. I used lots of paper but I did it. I'm beginning to dislike Dad... He takes MY CAR! Like it's his. He doesn't bother to take me out to practice for my road test yet he asks me if I'm going to go out driving. He knows I don't have my license yet. How in the fucking hell am I going out to drive my car. He asks me if he can take it to go and play lotto at 5:30 and doesn't come back until 3:00am drunk! I hate him!

Well it's only 3 more days to go... It doesn't seem like 1 year, seems like yesterday you were here. I miss you and I love you. In my letter to Etta, I told her about my rash, headaches, nauseous, chills etc. I'm seriously thinking again about getting tested. I'm still trying to come to terms with your death. I'm not afraid to die or at least I don't think so. Sometimes I really want to just be with you. Who's to say that if that should happen you would want to be with me? You might not even be there- wherever there might be. What if death is not what I think it is?

I'm not working, what a relief! I'm free to study acting, music and dance. I don't want the mundane 9-5 job. I want to enjoy my work for whatever time I have left...

The end of the world is so very near, I can feel it. People just don't realize what's about to take place. The Rapture, the Tribulation. They don't know that regardless of what happens or what people may say, you have to believe. Not just in your heart but with your soul that God sent his only begotten son, that whosoever believe in him shall not perish but have everlasting life.

Dae did you believe? Do I believe? I do!

I went to an audition for casting agent Eileen Hansford a commercial for G.E light bulbs. I was light bulb #2. She couldn't use me but gave me some advice. Why? Said I had to change my resume otherwise companies would throw it away. She also referred me to Tony & Maria Greco on camera acting class. Do I have the potential? Do I have the face of a naive, gullible young woman to be taken for her money? What have I got to lose?

Technically -$275.00. 8 weeks of my life to be doing other things? Being vulnerable, putting myself on the line? What have I got to gain? A chance to learn about myself. A chance to grow as an actress, get a commercial, make money. Lead to other things like getting an agent, to be happy because I'm doing what I've always dreamed? It's hard trying to analyze and put things into perspective. Not things but my life! I wanted to leave my job but wanted to get fired so I could collect unemployment. They wanted to fire me, instead Michael said no and gave me a promotion instead to Production Assistant. Finally, I asked again, relentlessly. The fired me. Went to unemployment the next day. Everything was easy. Wanted to work part time off the books. Smart move or what? Want to study and train with vocal coach Thurman Bailey. Want to take dance classes, acting classes and still audition. Vocal coach $40 hr., $130 ballet & jazz dance classes. Can't go to Lee Strasberg its $5,000. What will I do? What's the most important thing right now? Was going to take speech and movement class. Why? It will help me when I'm singing on stage. Then why am I auditioning as an actress? I can't afford to take classes for individual needs. So being realistic..

Work temp assignments for cash? Still collect unemployment. Take Commercial Acting class. Instead of paying $675 for dance, acting and voice which I don't have. Pay $275 for commercial class. It gets me started with basics of acting. If I get a commercial, WHEN- it could help me pay for dance and vocal lessons. In my other life was well off financially? It's going to take a lot of sacrificing and arguments but I don't care! When I do *make it "big" no one will be arguing then. No, they'll be happy and want a piece of the action.*

Daedalus, I don't only want to "make it" for me but I also want to make it for you because life wasn't fair for you. Who said it was, right? You didn't get your chance so I'll do it for the both of us. They say (they?) success is nothing without someone you love to share it with. Well this may sound crazy but I want to share it with you even in death! Even when I know you're not around... Are you? I still love you. Maybe I'm smothering you in death as I did when you were here. I can't seem to let go- at least not yet anyway! D-

Date?

In a way it's very well that I don't have lots of 'friends" It's time for me to pour myself into my career. Not half assed. I have no husband, boyfriend, children, and major responsibilities. I don't need so called 'friends" distracting me. I ask myself all the time, what do you want it? Do you want it? Are you willing to dedicate, sacrifice, and excel to get it? What do you have to do (without hurting people) to get it?

Dae you are alive to me in spirit. You are the strength that will guide me. You always believed in me as a person and artist. And for this alone I love you for it.... Thank you! With God & you behind me I know, I'll make it. D-

Date?

Its 6:30 am. It's getting light outside. Remember one particular sunrise I experienced. You were at school. It was so beautiful that I had to write to you and tell you about it, minute by minute. You showed me that the simple things are the most beautiful. I will watch this sunrise though since you've been gone I haven't noticed the sun at all...

And I will think of you! Every sunrise I see, I will think of you! I think maybe this is another step towards healing. What do you think? D-

Friday Feb 9th 2:04am

Elaine and I went to the village. She bought 2 pairs of shoes. We wanted to go to the movies but we couldn't find a cab. Fate? We got to the theatre at 11:30 and the last movie was 9:30 so we missed the movie. Fate? We didn't know what to do. Elaine suggested we get our tarot cards read. The name of the tarot card reader was Dee. Fate? She read Elaine first. People will be very jealous of her talent. Choose your friends wisely. She was a good sweet person who loved to have fun.

Will get married. Love & romance will hit in May.

Me: I will probably live to be 85 yrs. old, I'm smiling on the outside and hurting on the inside. When I get married it will be for keeps, no divorce. I'm very worried about something but not to, everything will be ok. I come from a good family but I'm not close to them. Someone I loved was taken away from me. I'm hurting because I'm grieving because I've been separated from a certain person. I will not be rich but I won't be poor. My career will make me travel to different places. She asked me what I did for a living.

First- yes I am worried. Am I healthy, do I have AIDS, am I going to die soon, will my career take off, will I survive not having a steady job, pursuing my career.

> *2nd- Yes I come from a good family and yes I'm not close to my dad and brother.*
> *3rd-Yes I'm smiling on the outside and hurting on the inside. I miss Dae terribly, I'm grieving,*
> *4th –Yes I was separated from someone I love. Daedalus*
> *5th- Yes I want to travel to Paris, Italy in July 6th Yes I will make it musically perhaps I won't be a millionaire but I'll live comfortably. What will the future really hold for me? Did she really know? Could she really see these things in me? What if everything she told me was the exact opposite? Yes, what if? That damned fate! I went to an audition. They called me back for a 2nd audition. They want to showcase me. Fate? Sometimes I get the feeling that I'm not well emotionally. Maybe I'm grieving too much? I wonder if Etta & Derrick received their card. The letter I wrote to them were very deep. They probably think I've lost it mentally. What was their reaction? My inquiring mind wants to know.*

As I continued my walk through the world without my best friend the ground beneath my feet still felt uneven. The sky had shifted and felt off-kilter. Valentine's Day is coming and I miss my love. I'm struggling. My body was thin. I had lost about 20 pounds. I was moody, withdrawn and uncommunicative. I had no interest in anything. I closed myself off like a pond that submerges a stone. I was feeling ages old and none the wiser.

February 14th 1989
It Valentine's Day. Daedalus 1 year angel anniversary.

I got a red rose from someone whom I love with all my heart. Not from my so called friends a single card. Nothing from Dad or Chris. I know who really cares. I know who really loves me. I just hope she know how much I love her. I would lay down my life for her. If I had to choose between my music and her, I'd never sing another note. I will love her until death do us part... Mom I love you sooo very much. I hope that you're as happy long after the world turns. You deserve it and I know you will find it. You probably don't realize but you are such a strong person emotionally and mentally. That's where my strength comes from. You and I are survivors against all odds. We're both so different but so much alike. I'm so proud to have you as my mother. I'll go through hell and high-water for you. Just a figure of speech: I don't really want to go to hell and I'm terrified of water but you know what I mean.
Your daughter Deirdre Louise-2/14/89

Dying, death, dead, passed away; words and phrases that forcefully connected with me. The inevitable destination of all living things. I thought of my own mortality. On this onerous day I felt oppressed beyond words and it was almost unbearable. It was hard to move through the world today. My feet were heavy like cinderblocks. With each laborious step I took, I felt the guilt of being alive and the feeling of abandonment.

Date?
I've been having dreams about people from my childhood. Tammy and family came to visit. We were still living at

767 Jefferson Ave. All I remember was she kept saying I'm pregnant, I'm pregnant. Also dreamt about Robert Dutton. 3 days later he called talking very religiously. I think he's is an evil person and I'll never ever trust him. I hate him. Whenever I talk with him I get flustered. He throws me out of sync. It's been 5 years. Why would he call now?

Had a very pleasant dream about Tim & Lisa. Tim and I finally went to bed together to see what it would have been like. Annette was in the dream too. We were all hanging out, partying, and having one hell of a time. Dreamt about Jane and feces. What could this mean?

March 9th,

Dae 42 year old Artist and Photographer Robert Mapplethorp died of AIDS complications.

March 20th 1989

Last night I had a dream. I was on a train which was travelling outside. (LIRR perhaps) It was full of people that I knew and we were very loud and rowdy. I look across the train and there were two people. One of them was Daedalus. He was talking to someone that had their back to me so I could only see the side of this persons face. They were talking in front of the big window. Daedalus turned to me and smiled. He was laughing and having a good time. He looked great. Like when I first met him. His face was aglow and he looked very healthy. He had on that famous leather jacket. Now I know that he's telling me that he's okay. He's happy, not to worry. Go on and live my life. Daedalus you will always have a special place in my heart. Love Always D-

April 5th, 1989
Dream: My old boss was there in the big auditorium with Oprah. Michael wanted us to do another show on drug use. (Cocaine). Other students were there from Music & Art. Some faces I used to hang out with in school and others who were seniors when I was a sophomore. I left. Got outside and was in midtown section of Manhattan somewhere bet 38th and 40's. Was walking around by myself. Few clouds.

Decided to walk to the Eastside by the Trump Towers. Saw large crowd of people who were going into the Cathedral. Heard someone say it was John F. Kennedy. I ended up sitting in some kind of court yard with a nun who was whittling a wood plaque with JFK's name on it. She was scraping up thin green pieces of a floor and spreading it on the plaque. Handy men came to fix the floor that she had taken the scrapings from.

Back amongst crowds of people. They're bringing JFK's body out of the church. People were crying. I started walking towards this parkway heading to Brooklyn. I ran into Al B Sure (who I can't stand). We knew each other. I didn't want to talk. His girlfriend caught up with us. They both had on fur coats. He asked me what I was reading. He said "Health, Beauty and Makeup"? His girlfriend said leave her alone. I read that book and it's very helpful and interesting.

Started walking again by myself. Was back in Manhattan looking in the windows of boutiques. Looked up and saw this store with the name Daedalus. It was closed. Don't know if it was out of business or just closed. What does this mean?

I don't think I smiled for over a year yet alone laughed. I think any laughter from me would have easily turned into madness and hysteria. I was just bidding my time. Waiting for the ground to open up and swallow me like a sink hole swallows up an entire house.

The summer stretched golden in front of me with its promises of beautiful sunrises along the New York Rivers and oceans. Why is it that life seemed so much more animated in the summertime? Is it because the days are longer? Summertime. In its spell, holds the assurances of kids shouting and laughing at picnics and barbeques. Even the clothes are louder! Then you have the sun shining brightly in the sky, beaming down, taunting those of us who are not having fun. Bustling crowds and fireworks waiting for the watercolor sunsets and warm summer nights. This new awareness made my senses of being without Daedalus sting like having my first glass of aged scotch.

Chapter *Twenty-Three*

*Only you hear my call
When you answer you soften my fall
Won't you stay, and we can a find a way
I don't know what you do
When I dream in the darkness with you
We could sway and dance the blues away
Sway and surrender to the motion
Sway to the music you feel as your body lets go
(Sway) in a world that's your own
At the end of the day we dance the blues away-Mica Paris
"Sway (Dance the Blues Away)"- ©UMC Universal*

June 23rd 1989 2:05 am
Haven't written in a while. Tonight or should I say today begins my fourth day in the Life Spring basic training course. Right now I'm doing an exercise, one hour of silence to think about what I experienced with the Black and White game but before I get to that...
Wed started the first day of my basic, well it actually started as soon as I enrolled at the guest event... Got there just in time to pay and register. Was calm, relaxed, eager, excited, curious, happy and doubtful. Doubtful because Elaine whose gone through the basic course told me about the process and a few of the games. Thursday I came to the conclusion that I only stand responsible for 90% of my life and that is why I'm not getting the results I want.

I also learned that I was being a victim and others were supporting me in this.

August 16th 1989
Daedalus -60 Year old Actress Amanda Blake died today. Although she had throat cancer at the time at her death, the T is- she contracted the HIV virus from her ex-husband and had died of AIDS related complications. Oh my god...

September 26th 1989 11:49pm
I haven't written for quite some time. There's so much to say, where do I start? Life Spring is over! Yes I didn't do the final course which is the LP or Leadership Program. I don't need to kid myself. I feel I won't ever take it but I'm still open to the possibilities (wink). Things are happening for me. I'm now in a relationship with someone. His name is Rick McMorrow who I met at a Comedy Show we both performed in at Brooklyn College. He is gorgeous, intelligent, talented, playful, strong, passionate, supportive, party animal, fun, powerful, honest and committed. (Life Spring terminology) I was very attracted to him since day one and still am. To be continued- have to get some sleep. 5 weeks ago started new job and working long hours. Exhausted!

Sunday October 16th 1989 2:09am
I met Rick at a comedy show we did at Brooklyn College. Originally he wasn't supposed to be in the show but to quote Life Spring- "there are no coincidences". The first time I saw him I was attracted to him. He has long brown hair with blonde highlights. He wears an earring, got a

great ass, and beautiful blue eyes. He's a Leo. We had an amazing, fun, fabulous time when we finally did the show. I told Elaine I was attracted to him but I didn't want to make the first move. We all hung out together a few times. He needed help moving from the upper west side so I let him borrow my car. That's when I told him that I was stuck on him. (Corny I know) He kissed me and it was confirmed. I was in love. For the 4th of July, we went to Far Rockaway Beach and chilled out until dark. We kissed and felt each other up the entire time. He was there, the day I graduated from my advanced Life spring course and I must say I looked and felt fabulous. He was house sitting for his lighting director friend Michael Franks. So we went back there to have the serious talk. I shared what I had just gone through with Daedalus and how he died. I told him that there was a possibility I could be infected. He looked at me, kissed me and said, that it was time I get tested. I knew we couldn't be intimate until I did. That next week I went to the PolyStuy clinic in the East Village.

All I could think about was how my life was going to change once I learned I was HIV-positive. The female counselor called me into a room and asked me some questions like "How will learning you are HIV-positive affect your mental health? How will it affect your sexual behavior? Who will you tell? What reactions do you anticipate?" You see, these hypothetical questions are supposed to help them assess whether a person is ready to learn if they are HIV-positive. They took a blood sample, they gave me my id number and said it would take about 4-6 weeks for the results to come back.

For the next 4 weeks Rick and I hung out but I was so worried about the results. What if? I ran over every scenario. How I would break the news if I was positive. The different reactions he would have.

What if I could never have sex again for fear of infecting someone? Finally week 5 rolled around and I got a call from the clinic to come in for my results. They suggested that I bring someone with me but the reality was I didn't have anyone. Or at least felt like I didn't have anyone to turn to and not feel judged. Another whole week went by and I still hadn't gone in to get my results.

Finally I was ready. It was a sunny day and warm out. Everything I saw, traffic, people, felt like they were moving in slow motion. I could hear my heart beating so loudly in my ears. The world felt very surreal. I walked into the clinic. Checked in at the desk and waited for them to call my number. Finally after about ten minutes of unmitigated terror, my number was called. I was led through a door into a tiny office. The counselor pulled out my file, paused for a second and then proceeded to give me my test results. No words. I had no words. I sat there for a minute. I couldn't believe it. I had tested negative for the antivirus. She told me that although it had been 2 yrs. since I was perchance exposed to the virus, it might not show up yet and I should get tested in another 6-8 months and subsequently from here on out. I was elated as I walked over to Michael's place to tell Rick the good news. Using protection, we made wild passionate love.

It's funny, I never thought there would be another after Dae but I was wrong... Rick, he makes my heart flutter, every time he kisses me I get butterflies. After a couple of months of us officially being together we got an apartment. Guess where? One of my favorite places in the world. THE VILLAGE!! 7 Jones Street between Bleecker and West 4th. Still auditioning, I took a job as office manager at a Proctologist doctor's office to pay the bills. I took the job because most of the patients were gay and was diagnosed with the virus. It was my way if staying connected to Daedalus and giving back. There was a co-worker of mine named Paul who was also positive. This job while it was a good idea in the beginning took its toll because I dealt with these clients all the time and when they got sick and couldn't show up for their appointments, I worried. I worried when their T-cell count dropped, or when I heard they were in the hospital for the first, second, third, fourth time. I had other friends who were, singers, dancers, actors and designers who were newly diagnosed, close to death or had died. It all became too much for me to bear. At the end of the year 1989, 149,902 are diagnosed with AIDS in the US, 89,817 are dead.

Chapter *Twenty-Four*

You took me riding in your rocket, gave me a star But
at a half a mile from heaven you dropped me back
Down to this cold, cold world
Took me riding in your rocket, gave me a star But
at a half a mile from heaven you dropped me back
Down to this cold, cold world.-Stevie Wonder
"Rocket Love" Stevie Wonder, © EMI Music Publishing, Sony/ATV
Music Publishing

Its 1990 and what I refer to as the years of wisdom and enlightenment stage of my life. Two years had passed since Feb 14th 1988 and for the first 18 months I was out of it. In the beginning I couldn't sleep or eat. I was losing weight and all I could do was grieve. The walks down to the beach soothed my pain a little. I had lost my smile, my joy and my sense of self was shaken to its core. Listening to music that we both loved hurt even more. Only talking to him helped some. I stopped going out with friends and in due course quit the singing group I was in. I was away from work for about four weeks. I wanted to curl up in a ball and die. My friends became worried about me. They kept trying to get me to go out but I said no to all invites. I raged. I raged at God and decided I was never going to open my heart up like that and love so hard again.

When people find out I'm a Buddhist they always ask what was it that made me choose Buddhism. What I had experienced over the last few years of my life was the catalyst. This is when I started to really contemplate religion and faith and what it really meant to me. Was it really in alignment with who I was, what I had been through, what my friends were going through and how I truthfully, honestly felt? I came to the stark realization and concluded that I didn't believe in GOD and thus began my researching of Buddhism.

1992-2013

You got to have fire,
You got to have passion,
Cuz if you wanna be with me,
You got to be Carefree-Mica Paris

Rick and I moved from the West Village to 57th Street & 9th Ave and we ended up going on tour together with a theatre company. I was blessed to have travelled all over the United States with another great love of my life. While on the road I heard that Larry Levan, the DJ extraordinaire who put the Paradise Garage on the map died from AIDS related illness. I was so sad and missed Daedalus at that very moment.

After being on the road for about four years Rick and I were engaged. We came back to New York and settled down in the East Village in 1996. Baby fever started to set in. I joined a band, started a few bands of my own and started acting again. In 1999, we moved to Harlem. They tried to harass Rick when we first moved there because he was a white boy but this ex-marine wasn't having. By the end of the 90's the love of my fucking life tells me he does not ever want to have kids. After 11years together, in 2001, I lose yet another lover and friend. We parted ways.

At the end of 1990's, 198,466 persons are diagnosed with AIDS in the US, 121,255 are dead.

February 14th 2013
It's after midnight. Well is officially 25 years since Daedalus left us. I just posted on FB like I've done the past few years to honor his memory. Today I posted this:
Daedalus,
Today I celebrate the life you lived and the blessing that you were to me during your time on Earth. I remember you. I feel you. I know you exist in my heart and elsewhere. I sip your favorite drink and taste the food you loved. The simple pleasures that are no longer yours, exchanged for the joy of being Home, knowing Truth, seeing ALL. I love you Daedalus. Today, in your honor, I celebrate Life!

February 16th 2013
For some reason it feels like I'm grieving Daedalus all over again. I've been thinking more about him this last year. Perhaps it's because I'm writing this story about our time together. Maybe it's brought up everything I felt about our time together all back to the surface. I'm lucky that I still have cassette tapes (funny shit) of our Rareform days. Cards from him to me, photos of him and his special message to me on tape. He shared a piece of his soul and I get to hear him speak it directly to me, hear him say he loves me and felt blessed to have me in his life. This Valentine's Day, felt so hard and horrible. I don't think I've missed him so much like this where I couldn't almost breathe. I found Etta via an internet search. Decided to write to her and tell her that I haven't

forgotten and how I still miss him and think about him all the time. And when I think about Dae, which is every day! I also sent her a copy of my demo CD and shared with her that "Autumn Leaves" is my song to Daedalus. To let her know I still remember and cherish Dae and the short time we had together. In celebration of his life, at work I listened to songs we danced to at the Paradise Garage back in the day. Went to my second post op check up with Dr. Pollack. Got a clean bill of health. My vocal cords are beautiful and pristine as he put it.

Went down to 8th Street, where we spent most of our time together. Most of the stores that we knew have long gone away. Went to Washington Square Park and sat in the cold and thought about Dae and the time we spent in this park. I remember me, him and Sec were there celebrating his birthday here. We bought him a birthday cake and Champaign. We smoked a joint and laughed and danced. Where we were in the park when we had a picnic and kissed for hours before we ended up at Riverside Drive Park where our baby was conceived. I kept having to take deep breaths so as not to totally break down in the park. Couples walking by. Snow melting everywhere. Daedalus I was trying to feel you, feel your spirit. Thought maybe this would help me with this Valentine's Day missing you sooo very much. In celebration of your life I went to Eva's on 8th street. Yes it's still there; and had a falafel in your honor. Walked over to Christopher Street past the Stonewall Inn and another gay bar. Walked past the Waverly diner which was one of our favorite spots and though of you/ us. Came home, listened to your taped message to me as I do every year and cried for you. Cried because I miss you and your beautiful complicated self.

Feb 16th 2013
Daedalus,
As I sit here in my apartment on this Saturday afternoon at 3:50pm on Feb 16th 2013. I still cry for you for us. It's been 25 years since you left your body on this earth. I still count your birthdays. This May you would've been 50. Wow what a party you would've had. I count each day that passes and re-live the hours leading up to the morning you died and the day's afterwards. I know it seems masochistic but I don't know what else to do. How else to be when I'm missing you. Is this healthy? We had some beautiful times and tumultuous times together. Passionate relationships. TOGETHER! We had them together. Together, together, together. People are living with AIDS now much better and longer due to the advance in medicine. I believe a cure is around the corner. It hit people all over the world. Africa, women, seniors. Women can have babies today even if they are positive. If we only had this medical knowledge when you and I were going to have a baby... but we didn't know. We just didn't know. News just recently arrived that now with rigorous prenatal care and treatment by educated and experienced providers, that the chance that a mother living with HIV could spread the virus to her baby was now less than 2 percent. Because there are effective, tolerable HIV meds, it makes it possible for parents to watch their children grow into adulthood and beyond. While this is great news for the world, for me it was also a bittersweet reality. Dae, I hope you're okay with me

telling our love story, sharing it with the world. I'm compelled. What do you think of our first Black President? I and my girlfriends went to the first inauguration in 2009. Wouldn't you know he got re-elected? I remember standing in the cold morning air on the Washington Mall thinking about you.

I reached out to your sister April on Facebook. We left each other messages a couple of times but that's it. So what do you think of this social media and internet thing? Oh how you would love Smart Phones, iPods and laptops. I remember you had this bright yellow Walkman when I first met you that day at Bloomie's. You missed Discman for CD's. Now you can keep 1,000+ songs on a device that's portable and smaller and thinner than a baseball card or a little bigger than a piece of gum. OMG- I know!!!

I'm still singing and think of you every time I step out on stage. I don't get to dance much. Most of the men I've met can't dance worth shit, but when I do it's a time that I feel free, uninhibited and beautiful and I think of you/us dancing together at the clubs. I miss that!

Funny how every guy I've dated since you couldn't dance to save their lives. They have all been awful dance partners. Would love to have my next friend/ lover enjoy going out to dance.

I have never been married, no children, although I wanted them... Why am I stuck in the past? Dae am I stuck in the past? Or is this me grieving because I'm writing our story? Is this survivor's guilt? Is

this normal? Is this why I'm single, never married? Am I stuck emotionally, psychologically? No I'm not stuck in the past, I just miss you!

Beyoncé is coming on tonight. I think you would've loved her! Diva extraordinaire! Can sing her ass off. Daedalus, we lost Luther.
Michael & Whitney are gone too.
I stopped believing in God after you died. But my spiritually is so strong. I've been a Buddhist for the last 12 years. I chant for you along with our baby that we never got to know.
Dae can you hear me when I talk to you? Can you feel me, the love I have for you? Are you with me? Show me? Send me a sign. When I hear specific songs that we both knew and loved is that you? When I see items that you loved like Castile peppermint soap, is that you?
I search for you in my dreams but I can't find you. I look for you in the little white butterflies that seem to follow me. Is that you? Have you been here with me all along? If so, show me! Let me feel you! Let me see you! While sitting in Washington Square Park on your Valentine's Day Memorial Day, some stranger (you perhaps?) gave me a Valentine's Day card. It said "Greetings Stranger! I don't normally do these random acts of kindness (although I should more often) but today I felt inspired by you and wanted to let you know that you are loved, you are cherished, and you are special. Let's make a pact and tell our neighbors we love them just because. Have a wonderful day you! Sincerely, Anonymous Friend. Happy Valentine's Day!

Sunday March 2, 2013 11:39pm
Crazy feelings these past few months. Haven't felt like myself in quite a while. Sitting in Au bon Pain having chamomile tea waiting to go to my 12pm vocal session

with David. Pretty much cried this entire weekend. Not sure if its anxiety, depression sadness or what. I'm feeling tired of living lately. Even looked up on the internet about suicide. I gave Beverly my old therapist a call on Friday for some help. Meeting with her on Wed. Haven't spoken to mom and dad since my surgery in December. They both make me so sad in how they continue to treat each other, me caught in the middle. They have no love or respect for each other and it breaks my heart. It seems as though I've been grieving Daedalus all over again and it's been 25 years. I finally found an address for his mom Etta. I sent her a letter along with a card and my CD. I wish Dae would visit me in my dreams. I so desperately need to see, feel him. I feel it's the only thing that will give me some relief. Life really sucks right now!

April 16th 1:27am

Woke up! Just met Dae in my dreams! Thank you. Thank you Daedalus. Thank you for visiting me and comforting me, for reaching out to me! It's a mystery. Not sure how it all happens and don't really care. Dream: Was at an awards ceremony. Oprah was on the large stage speaking and presenting. Guests were over to the side in the lounge area. Some were sitting on this round sofa in a circle. Some were dressed in gowns and some had on jeans. Saw this girl with natural hair, in jeans with her feet up. She stood out to me. She was very relaxed. Someone asked her a question as people in the center were speaking about their life. Next we're sitting in a circle at night on a beach in front of a bonfire, talking. Someone asked me a question... I don't remember what the question was but I gave 4 answers to the enquirer. 1st reply was yoga, 2nd *answer was meditation & acupuncture, 3rd answer confidence, 4th love- self-love. I look up and was there on the beach sitting in the sand facing Daedalus. We were doing some sort of ritual with our hands, holding each other in front of the fire. Face to face, fire crackling. Palms touching, hands clasped, my heart was filled with love. He stood up to go inside to check the big metal pot boiling on the stove. I followed him in the door to the kitchen. He opened the cabinet and took out spices to put into the boiling pot. He was making candy out of vegetables. He smiled at me. I felt at ease. Home. The house felt familiar but didn't look familiar. Walls were beige & white. Walked through the kitchen down 2 steps into the living room. There was a mantel piece on my left and there was a photograph of me and him. But it was me in pigtails. Kind of like my second grade school photo of me in pigtails and the sky blue dress. I said to him wow, I can't believe I was 20 yrs. old in that photo but looked 8. He said you weren't 20 you were 30. There were 2 doors. One to my right and the other door right in front of me. I wondered which door was my room. Didn't have a chance to go through one of the doors because I woke up. Thank you Daedalus for your visit into my dreams. I've been wanting this for sooo long. It felt good. Daedalus thank you, for hearing me, for loving me, for comforting me. Thank you for letting me love you. Thank you for allowing me to be my best self! Please continue visiting me in my dreams as often as you can. With love in my heart for you always- Deirdre*

Every now and again as I continued to write I got a little anxious about revealing so much about me and my life and how this endeavor would be judged. But, after being diagnosed with vocal polyps, having the surgery and during my healing process having to spend time in total vocal silence I had a realization of what a gift this actually was. It afforded me the opportunity to be still. I was able to sit and reflect on who I was, wanted to be, what I wanted and what I needed. This was my wakeup call to own, live and speak my truth. With that said I decided to share all of it. Well most of it. There are a few things that I choose not to recount in our story and probably never will. I still want to keep a few things that Dae and I shared just between the two of us.

It's amusing, startling and wonderful to be able to hear and see my twenty year old self again in these pages. Oh how very brave she was. And so, to honor and cherish that twenty year old is the reason why I decided not edit any of my journal entries grammatically or otherwise. I didn't want to water down her voice technically or emotionally. I wanted the reader to see, hear and feel her.

Penning this book has been liberating to my soul. I remain grateful for my second, third, fourth and fifth chances of trying to get it right. My life is not perfect by any stretch of the imagination and I still have to work at staying motivated and focused towards fulfilling my dreams. I see each day as a fresh chance to forge ahead. I'm also appreciative for all of the opportunities good, bad or indifferent that show up in my life. I am still that dreamer from Brooklyn. And you do know that successful dreamers never give up hope right? I keep hope alive with the self-assurance that no matter what, I will meet new challenges head-on and with optimism. I refuse to give up the hope that my dreams and even my life, will turn out well. As for the bumps and bruises along the way, I am soothed and continue healing by remaining open and encouraged. Sharing my pain gave it meaning by the very act of expressing it. My tenderness comes from that pain. I'm amazed and delighted that I still have the capacity to give and receive love.

July 11th 2013
Daedalus still speaks to me to let me know he's still with me. Why just last night while doing edits on the part where we went to the movies to see Crocodile Dundee. Guess what movie was playing on TV when I woke up this morning at 6am. Yes, Crocodile Dundee was just beginning on channel 218. I smiled and silently said good morning to him and thanked him for a sign of his presence.

My reality of moving forward with my life has been full of hits and misses in regards to relationships, music, acting, jobs, and spirituality and in 1989 I made a choice to explore Buddhism even deeper.

Some people are shocked and a bit bothered that although is been 28 years and I've been in a number of relationships since then, that I still think about Daedalus and miss him tremendously. But I put forth this question to those cynics; since when does moving on means forgetting someone and the life that you shared with them? Some people have implied or expect that once a person grieves and moves on, the deceased person of the life you previously lived is somehow supposed to fade into oblivion; due to the fact that the ones left behind, have made a new life with a new love. And is apparently never again supposed to be sad or wistful because their late beloved is no longer here. For a while I functioned in life with grief and sadness. At my core I thought and felt that loving again would dishonor or disrespect the memory of Daedalus. However, I know that I wasn't destined to remain alone and longing for a life that was no longer here to live. We all have an infinite capacity to love. Loving again does not mean that the love for a late beloved somehow goes away. It just doesn't. This is a concept that a fair amount of people just can't wrap their minds around.

The fact is, that even in a wonderful new life, things like holidays, birthdays, anniversaries, "angelversaries" (the date of a beloveds death) and the happening of various life milestones can all serve as painful reminders that someone whom you have loved is no longer here to celebrate, witness and in general, be a part of a life that was built with love.

It really doesn't matter that it's been 28 years since losing one of the great loves of my life. I can tell you without reservation that I still love him and I still treasure the life and all of the messiness that we had together. Nevertheless, I also moved forward into a beautiful new life. Neither forgetting nor betraying my past. My grief and recovery were slow and steady as it moved into a life of my own design. A design that happily included new loves and new adventures to go along with that love.

So you see, the love that you have for your late beloved will never go away. Not ever. Not with the passage of time. Not with the introduction of a new person into your life and into your heart. And certainly not with 8 gajillion people around you saying things like, "Well- you should be over it by now". I know that loving again does not imply lack of or the end of love from the past. I understand that I am not destined to remain in mourning forever... that isn't why I'm here.

No matter how deep my grief became, gradually I got pulled back into the world; perhaps even against my will. At times it certainly felt like I was going one step forward then two steps back. It's funny though. Life has a way of throwing moments our way that wake us up to the possibilities still in front of us.

There are not a lot of people who know this particular slice of my life and the few that I chose to tell I will be forever grateful. I remember all the people who helped me through my grieving and allowed me to talk about Daedalus over and over and over. One special person comes to mind. Elaine P. She was this young, hip, cool, talented fashion designer at Gordon Henderson showroom where I worked after Dae passed. Elaine was one of the creative minds of the GH Team. Her sketches for each new season were gorgeous, whimsical and sophisticated. She had been through some traumatic things herself and trusted me with her secrets. E had a beautiful mind and spirit, a contagious laugh and genuinely cared about people. She didn't judge me and my relationship with Daedalus. She embodied compassion and understanding. While she was already a remarkable artist she also began exploring photography at the time and had a wonderful eye and flair when it came to this medium. I remember hanging in her little apartment in Park Slope and she would get to cooking her amazing pot of chilly and we would just smoke our cigarettes, drink wine or coffee and share our life experiences with each other.

Because I was missing Dae so much I didn't even want to be in New York or the entire United States. My heartache was that unbearable that I wanted to leave the country. We decided that one day we'd relocate to Paris, France. We would open up a cafe where I would sing and she would discover the neighborhoods and its inhabitants and take beautiful pictures and display them in the café and sell them.

Well, I finally did arrive in Paris but it was decades later. While standing underneath the Eifel Tower on a sunny but cold day in April I thought of her. While enjoying some jazz one night at the Autour de Midi-Minuit in Montmartre, I thought of her and our dream and smiled inwardly to myself.

I realized that I was standing inside of the legacy of who I was and whom I had become was an enhanced, enriched version of me. I was myself!

EPILOGUE

You have given so much to me, A chance to find my destiny
Feeling is believing, And I'm feeling fine
Fine despite the things I know, There is no place I'd rather go
Or be here is my destiny, And now's the time for
Sittin' in the middle of the ones I love-Nothing else matters
Sittin' in the middle of the ones I love-Surrounded by their light
Sittin' in the middle of the ones I love-Nothing can shatter
This notion in my mind that all we do
Will fade away in time but I'll remember you-Raul Midon
"Sittin' In The Middle", Raul Sterling Midon - © Fintage Pub & Collection B.V.

Today I sit in the space of enlightenment and peace.

Enlightenment

As I work on this piece of my life story "Deirdre & Daedalus: No Ordinary Love", some days are harder than others when it comes to writing. I often wonder how his family, my family would feel about me writing this? There will be people who don't want to hear the pain faced by an uninfected individual. Some won't care to know, understand or want to re-live the severity of the impact this AIDS epidemic had in our lives. Some will try to deny and minimize this story every step of the way. Some will discount that this epidemic left a population of survivors who were left to walk the earth like robots or zombies. Telling ourselves and others that everything's fine while we were actually numb, cut off from our emotions and entrenched in a state of denial.

After Dae passed, I watched friends, lovers, and colleagues sicken and die. My spirit shifted from being in a state of simple grief to multiple loss to compounded repeated trauma, without awareness or self-knowledge. Was this what fighting in a war felt like? The circuits of emotion within me became strangely redirected and sometimes entirely disconnected.

I lost Ricky, John, Rayford, Paul, Jane. Other friends and acquaintances would die and I would feel nothing. I crashed under the weight of so much sickness and death. Funerals ceased to serve as a gathering for all of us left behind as an event to help soothe the pain. I wasn't alone in what seemed to be a perversion of internal responses. You see, at the AIDS memorial marches and displays of the NAMES Project quilt, I watched visitors engaging in social banter, gossiping, joking, doing anything except confronting the direct experience of grief. But I don't fault them. Perhaps that's all they had in them to get through that day, those hours, minutes, seconds.

No one ever says to survivors of an earthquake that they are wrong for being profoundly shaken by the experience. We survivors, of this epidemic were overwhelmingly traumatized. We experienced depression, anxiety, panic attacks and listlessness. I know, that because of their religious beliefs, some won't care. Nevertheless, it doesn't matter because again it's MY story! Mine and Daedalus'!

Peace

When I first met Daedalus, I thought for a split second he might be gay but it never really mattered much because acceptance was acceptance to me. Unconditional meant unconditional to me. All the same, as we got to spend more and more time together for our music projects, there definitely was a sexual chemistry brewing between us. We were both outgoing yet sensitive, passionate and we both loved music, theatre and dance. Friends would say they could feel the charge of attraction between us. How we delighted in the flirtations, the cheeky dialogue, the sexual innuendo on and off the dance floor and the intrigue of it all.

Then, that one night, changes the trajectory of my life forever. He shows up at my house and tells me he attracted to me and he loves me. A few weeks later we slept together. That day on the terrace when he told me his truth after our night of partying. So while I was attracted to him, I figured he would just be one of my gay best friends. Let's just say that he did not act like a gay best friend usually acts. In fact, he seemed more comfortable with my body than some of the straight men I had dated.

It was always my belief that, if someone is having sex with both women and men, then he is perhaps behaviorally bisexual, regardless of what he says his orientation is. However, at that moment in time he chose me and I chose him. At the end of the day his sexuality didn't come up in our daily lives.

Now, I did question it at first. I questioned myself. Was it possible I could feel this cool about all of it? That I could really love him the way I did? That this relationship could feel this good; I was this into him? But then again it was the way he held me close to him. How he treated me. I didn't feel like he had the need to consume me or the need to want to rescue me or judge me.

Being together with him always felt like waves rushing over me. It wasn't planned; love snuck up on me. I was in it and I wasn't going to let him go.

When it comes to relationships, no matter whom you're involved with or dating, part of loving someone is taking that leap into the unknown and the only way to be truly sure, is over span of time. It also depends on the values of the person, the strength of their commitment and whether both partners want to work at it. Yes, we were a bit more open-minded than most couples but the amount of honesty developed at the beginning of our relationship served us well.

No one really made a big deal about us. We knew not everyone would be as supportive as our circle of friends. To be honest, we had zero interest in hanging out and talking with someone who thought our relationship was a sham. Anyway, we ran with a pretty artsy, eclectic crowd.

Bottom line, I was in love. I loved this young man. It was the way he moved. His energy. His intelligence. His creativity, His self-expression. It was the way I felt around him. He brightened my day. There was no one like him. I remember his hands; beautiful, long, expressive, and dramatic. He was hungry for life and thirsty for the freedom to live it on his own terms. I remember that smile. I remember his laugh. His laugh could be wild, sweet, playful, mischievous and seductive. The sound of his laughter. The kind of laugh that was contagious. I can summon up the timbre of his speaking voice. The affectation in the enunciation of his words flowed as if he were on stage reciting Shakespeare. I remember that tenor singing voice and the occasional angelic falsetto he would use. I remember his eyes. His big, brown, beautiful soulful eyes. I remember the sound of his beating heart when I laid my head on his chest. I remember his lips; full and luscious, soft and velvety.

My love for him was stronger than my pride. We gave each other the kiss of life. What we had was not perfect by any means. The more we got to know each other, the more our relationship plunged, grew, flowed and swelled. Our good times came and went. I don't believe our love was at all wrong. I wanted Daedalus and he wanted me. End of story. Yes, the relationship we had was no ordinary love. We believed what *we* believed. We gave each other all that we had to give of ourselves at that particular moment in time. I also believe something mysterious and heavenly lead us to each other. There was a bridge built from my heart to his. The way we came together felt natural. In the words of Joseph Campbell, we followed our bliss.

As Daedalus wasted away, the innocent days of our youth slowly began to vanish like one of the many beautiful sunsets that we'd watch together. Dissolving into the darkness of night; leaving behind remnants of joy and disaster. I often wonder if this grief will ever let me go. Any ordinary day brings it all about. Will this heartache ever be gone? Probably not. There's nothing anyone has said or can ever say to take this hurt and sadness away.

In my quite moments of meditation or chanting I feel overwhelming gratitude for having known him. What's more is, I feel his energy. I feel him near when I'm running around the city, stumbling upon the many places we use to go, smiling inwardly. This is perhaps the most bittersweet part of all.

With these wonderful memories comes with it the sorrow. Sorrow. Funny, this is actually the literal translation of my Celtic name Deirdre.

For many years after he died I walked around wearing the scar of un-forgiveness, at myself and at God for Daedalus dying and leaving me all alone. For saying to him he wasn't fighting hard enough. I carried the blemish of me not making amends before it was too late. When he died I was in the wilderness, lost without him. He was in the music. In the notes of the songs I could no longer bring myself to sing. But somewhere in my sadness I knew that I couldn't completely fall apart although I had every reason to come undone.

My scabs are healing. That war of anger and un-forgiveness no longer rages inside of me. It has been tempered with maturity, wisdom, growth and spiritual evolution. You never know what destiny is going to send your way. You just have to live in the moment. That's what it really is about. Just create special moments because that's what really lasts.

I never blamed him. Daedalus. We passionately fought with each other off and on until the end because we both loved each other but were so afraid. He tried to push me away to try and spare me and I couldn't reveal my pain and fear to him because I didn't want him to be broken by the burden of me becoming sick. He allowed me to love him. Every aspect of him. All of him. And in this allowing is when I came to truly know myself. My higher self.

As the disease ravished his mind and body I couldn't just walk away. I wouldn't walk away. I loved him until the end. I loved this young man so much that I surrendered everything within me and whispered those words to him. Telling him it was okay to go if he wanted. To go on and take flight.

After all this time and after all that's said and done I still love him. Because it *was* all about our love and so shall it be forever. Never ending.

Music Lyrics Copyright Acknowledgments

- Papa Loved to Love Me" Ledisi ©2003 LeSun Records
- "The Way" Meshell N'degeocello © Warner/Chappell Music, Inc.
- "Voices" Music & Lyrics by Deirdre L. Hall ©Red-Ride Music LLC.
- "Thine Own Self Be True" Music and Lyrics by Deirdre L. Hall" ©Red-Ride Music LLC.
- '"Ebony Eyes"- Stevie Wonder © Jobete Music Co. Inc.
- The Five Stairsteps "Ooh Child" Songwriters Vincent, Stan-Published by Lyrics © EMI Music Publishing, Sony/ATV Music Publishing LLC
- Rabindranath Tagore 1861–1941 was a Bengali poet, philosopher, social reformer, and dramatist who came into international prominence when he was awarded the Nobel Prize for literature in 1913. "Music is the purest form of art; therefore true poets seek to express the universe in terms of music. The singer has everything within him. The notes come out from his very life. They are not materials gathered from outside."

Copyright © 2020 Inspiring Quotes
https://www.inspiringquotes.us/quotes/kMR4_6LBx9yuS

- "Age of Aquarius" Fifth Dimension 1967 musical Hair -Aquarius/let The Sunshine In" written by James Rado ,Gerome Ragni Galt, MacDermot

- HTTP://WWW.SOKAHUMANISM.COM/NICHIRENBUDDHISM/CHRISTIANITY_AND_SGI_NICHIREN_BUDDHISM.HTML SEPTEMBER 5, 2014
- "A Love Supreme"-John Coltrane-Jowcol Music [BMI], © 1964 MCA Records, Inc
- Rūmī, in full Jalāl al-Dīn Rūmī, also called by the honorific Mawlānā, (born c. September 30, 1207, Balkh [now in Afghanistan]—died December 17, 1273, Konya [now in Turkey]), the greatest Sufi mystic and poet in the Persian language, famous for his lyrics and for his didactic epic Masñavī-yi Maʿnavī ("Spiritual Couplets"), which widely influenced mystical thought and literature throughout the Muslim world.- "You are the entire ocean, and the entire ocean is contained in each drop, expressing itself as each drop. We can allow everything to be as it is and find that there's this natural intuitive movement within us to flow this way or that, as if we have an inner sense of what the next step is and how to respond spontaneously in any moment. No rules. Just natural flow.

Simple. Light. Ease." ©2020 Encyclopedia Britannica, Inc. https://www.britannica.com/biography/Rumi
- "Break My Stride" by Matthew Wilder, Greg Prestopino © Universal Music Publishing Group, BMG Rights Management
- "Girls Just Want To Have Fun…- Cyndi Lauper Copyright: Sony/ATV Tunes LLC, Warner-Tamerlane Publishing Corp., Rellla Music Corp.
- You Light Up My life" by Debbie Boone Songwriter: Joe Brooks © Sony/ATV Music Publishing LLC, Warner Chappell Music, Inc, Universal Music

Publishing Group, BMG Rights Management, Mike Curb Music

- "Glamorous Life" Sheila E. Songwriters: Prince Rogers Nelson © Universal Music Publishing Group Copyright: WB Music Corp.
- The Greatest Love Of All- Whitney Houston Songwriters: Linda Creed / Michael Masser © Sony/ATV Music Publishing LLC
- What Have You Done For Me Lately-Janet Jackson Songwriters: James Harris Iii / James Samuel Iii Harris / Terry Lewis © Kobalt Music Publishing Ltd.
- Alton McClain & Destiny "It Must Be Love" Lyrics © Universal Music Publishing Group, Spec-O-Lite Music, Writers: David Allan Stewart, Bob Geldof
- Sade "The Sweetest Taboo" -Martin Ditcham, Helen Adu © Sony/ATV Music Publishing LLC
- Madonna "Live To Tell"-Madonna Ciccone, Patrick Leonard ©Warner/Chappell Music, Inc., EMI Music Publishing
- I Just Can't Stop, Loving You-- Michael Jackson MiJac Music © Sony/ATV Music Publishing LLC
- "War Of The Heart"- Sade, Stuart Matthewman / Helen Adu © Sony/ATV Music Publishing LLC
- "These Dreams" Heart Songwriters George Martin, Bernie Taupin, © Universal Music Publishing Group
- "Time After Time"- Cyndi Lauper/ Robert Hyman © Sony/ATV Music Publishing LLC, Warner/Chappell Music, Inc.

- You are My Heaven Roberta Flack & Donny Hathaway, Songwriters Eric Mercury, Stevie Wonder, ©Jobete Music Co. Inc.
- "Condition Of The Heart"- Prince Rogers Nelson ©Controversy Music
- "Fear"- Sade Songwriters Sarah Mclachlan, Stuart Matthewman, Helen Adu, © Tyde Music, Sony/ATV Songs LLC, Angel Music Ltd.
- No Plans for the Future- by Natalie Cole Songwriters: C. Jackson / M. Yancy © Universal Music Group
- Mary Wants to Be a Superwoman Stevie Wonder UMG (on behalf of Motown); UMPI, UNIAO BRASILEIRA DE EDITORAS DE MUSICA - UBEM, LatinAutor, LatinAutor - SonyATV, ASCAP, EMI Music Publishing, SOLAR Music Rights Management, CMRRA, and 6 Music Rights Societies
- "Haunt Me", Sade Songwriters Stuart Matthewman, Helen Adu, ©: Angel Music Ltd.
- "Sway (Dance the Blues Away)"-Mica Paris ©UMC Universal
- "Rocket Love" Stevie Wonder, © EMI Music Publishing, Sony/ATV Music Publishing
- Carefree-Mica Paris Songwriter Paul Draper Licensed to YouTube by

Reservoir Media Management (Label) (on behalf of Chrysalis Records); UNIAO BRASILEIRA DE EDITORAS DE MUSICA - UBEM, Abramus Digital, BMG Rights Management (US), LLC, LatinAutor, SOLAR Music Rights Management, ARESA, LatinAutor - UMPG, and 2 Music Rights Societies

- "Sittin' In The Middle", Raul Sterling Midon - © Fintage Pub & Collection B.V.

NOL REFERENCE INDEX

- Daedalus, Greek mythology
- Deirdre, Celtic mythology
- Children Conceived from Rape (CCR)
- Roe v. Wade
- Ryan Bomberger
- Ledisi's "Papa Loved to Love Me."
- Representative Todd Akin of Missouri
- Indiana State Treasurer and U.S. Senate nominee Richard Mourdock "something that God intended"
- Musician, Singer and Artist, Michelle N'degeocello has a song titled "The Way"
- Pablo Picasso Blue Period
- the Pig Pen character in Charlie Brown
- US combat troops arrive in Vietnam and by the end of the year, 190,000
- Rev. Dr. Martin Luther King, Jr., and more than 2,600 others arrested in Selma, Ala., during demonstrations against voter-registration rules.
- Black-nationalist leader Malcom X was shot to death at a rally in Harlem. Black people had been rioting for six days in the Watts section of Los Angeles: 34 dead, over 1,000 injured, nearly 4,000 arrested.
- President Johnson gets the Voting Rights Act of 1965 passed quickly in response to the violent events in Selma Alabama
- Academy Award went to My Fair Lady for Best Picture.

- Grammy Awards went to The Girl from Ipanema for Best Song and Hello, Dolly for Best Album.
- In the fall on 1965, the number-one hit song in the U.S. I Hear a Symphony by The Supremes as compiled by Billboard Hot 100 (November 14 to 27, 1965).
- Rabindranath Tagore-QUOTE
- Bhagavad-Gita on Hinduism
- L. Ron Hubbard.
- Louise Hay,
- Patricia Moreno,
- Daisaku Ikeda,
- Wayne Dyer,
- Oprah Winfrey,
- Esther Hicks,
- Marianne Williamson,
- Immaculee Illibagiza,
- Ishmael Beah,
- Joseph Campbell,
- Marianne Pearl,
- Maya Angelou,
- Tina Turner.
- Dylans Candy Store
- High School of Music & Art/Fiorello LaGuardia
- Irene Cara
- Performing Arts Jennifer Aniston, Ellen Barkin, Richard Benjamin, Julie Bovasso*, Adrien Brody, Charles Busch, Thom Christopher, Victor Cook, Keith David, Michael DeLorenzo, Dom DeLuise*, Thom Christopher, Dagmara Dominczyk, Omar Epps, Sarah Michelle Gellar, Cliff Gorman*, Jackee Harry, Anna

Maria Horsford, Paula Kelly, Hal Linden, Priscilla Lopez, Sonia Manzano, Janet Margolin*(Annie Hall, Ghost Busters, Murder She Wrote) , James Moody(Fame, D.C. Cab, Bad Boys, New York Undercover, Law & Order, The Best Man, The Last Dragon) Keith Nobbs (New York Undercover, The Sopranos, Law & Order, and Law & Order: Criminal Intent) Al Pacino (The Godfather, Scarface, Dog Day Afternoon, Any Given Sunday, Angels in America, Serpico) Sarah Paulson (Studio 60 on the Sunset Strip, Game Change, Martha Marcy May Marlene, and American Horror Story.) Elizabeth Peña (Rush Hour, Free Willy Boston Public, Without a Trace, CSI-Miami)   Brock Peters*(Porgy & Bess, To Kill A Mockingbird, Star Trek-Deep Space Nine), Suzanne Pleshette*(Alfred Hitchcock- The Birds, Bob Newhart), Tony Roberts(Woody Allen's-Annie Hall, Radio Days, Stardust Memories, Hannah and Her Sisters, A Midsummer Night's Sex Comedy, The Taking of Pelham One Two Three. Serpico, Amityville 3-D) Jennifer Salt, Helen Slater as Ruthless People, The Secret of My Success, and City Slickers, Smallville, The Lying Game.) Wesley Snipes (Michael Jackson's Bad video, Mo Better Blues, Jungle Fever, New Jack City, White Men Can't Jump,) Susan Strasberg* (The Virginian, The Invaders, Bonanza, The Streets of San Francisco, Night Gallery, McCloud, The Big Valley, Remington Steele, The Rockford Files). Glynn Turman (Cooley High, Hero Aint Nothin But a Sandwich, Five On the Black Hand Side, A Different World, Buffalo Solider, The Wire) Jessica Walter (Play Misty for Me, Columbo, Arrested Development)   Marlon Wayans

(I'm Gonna Git You Sucka, The Wayans Bros., Scary Movie, Scary Movie 2, White Chicks, Little Man, Dance Flick, Requiem for a Dream, G.I. Joe: The Rise of Cobra) Billy Dee Williams(Mahogany, Lady Sings the Blues, Star Wars Episode V: The Empire Strikes Back, Star Wars Episode VI: Return of the Jedi. Northern Calloway* (David- Sesame Street, A Mid-Summers Night Dream, Pippin), Jackee Harry (227, Sister Sister, Women of Brewster Place, Amen), Entertainers/Musicans/Singers, Hip Hop Artists Lyricists/Songwriters : Dana Dane, Lisa Fischer, Ben Harney, Janice Ian, Nikki Minaj, Alicia Keys,: Eartha Kitt*, Shari Lewis*, Melissa Manchester, Liza Minnelli, Peter Nero, Laura Nyro*, Felix Pappalardi, Freddie Prinze*, Slick Rick, Paul Stanley,Suzanne Vega, Ben Vereen, Eric Weissberg, Peter Yarrow, Carole Bayer Sager, Marilyn Bergman.

- The New York City Mayor Fiorello H. LaGuardia started the high school in 1936,
- The Tudors" actor Jonathan Rhys Meyers, reminded me of
- Erasmus Hall Music HS located in Brooklyn. Notable alumni would be Clive Davis, Stephanie Mills, Barbra Streisand,
- "You Light Up My Life" by Debbie Boone
- Avery Fischer Hall in Lincoln Center
- 1985 VH1 has just debuted, Prince is on his Purple Rain Tour,
- Apple and IBM are the only two serious players in the personal computer market,

- Compact discs before the common term CD's were being used, although they were becoming popular, they still hadn't quite caught on yet.
- Mafia Boss Paul Castellano is shot on orders of John J. Gotti.
- Riots and protests continue in Townships in South Africa against apartheid policies.
- Harlequin Studios
- Ziegfeld Follies were popular in the mid 1930's
- The Greatest Love of All. By Whitney Houston
- Janet Jackson "What Have You Done for Me Lately"
- Bard College
- Washington Square Park
- Riverside Drive Park
- Waverly Diner
- Brooklyn Heights
- Paradise Garage
- Danceteria
- Eva's Restaurant
- KS -Kaposi's sarcoma
- PCP also known as Pneumocystis pneumonia
- GRID
- Elizabeth Glaser
- HIV
- AIDS
- CD4 T-Helper Cells, diagnosis of transition to AIDS is usually confirmed by CD4+ T cell counts
- Toxoplasmosis, HIV Encephalopathy Tuberculosis,
- Non-Hodgkin's Lymphoma,
- Peripheral Neuropathy,

- Herpes Simplex,
- Candidiasis,
- Cytomegalovirus.Mayo Clinic Diseases and Conditions Cytomegalovirus (CMV) infection
- http://www.mayoclinic.org/diseases-conditions/cmv/basics/definition/con-20029514

Cytomegalovirus (CMV) infection
By Mayo Clinic Staff
Apr. 04, 2014

References

1. Cytomegalovirus (CMV) and congenital CMV infection: Overview. Centers for Disease Control and Prevention. http://www.cdc.gov/cmv/overview.html. Accessed Dec. 12, 2013.
2. Demmler-Harrison GJ, et al. Cytomegalovirus infection and disease in newborns, infants, children and adolescents. http://www.uptodate.com/home. Accessed Dec. 12, 2013.
3. Neurological consequences of cytomegalovirus infection information page. National Institute of Neurological Disorders and Stroke. http://www.ninds.nih.gov/disorders/cytomegalic/cytomegalic.htm. Accessed December 12, 2013.
4. Caliendo AM. Approach to the diagnosis of cytomegalovirus infection. Centers for Disease Control and Prevention. http://www.cdc.gov/cmv/overview.html. Accessed Dec. 12, 2013.
5. Sheffield JS, et al. Cytomegalovirus infection in pregnancy. http://www.uptodate.com/home. Accessed Dec. 12, 2013.

6. Friel TJ. Epidemiology, clinical manifestations and treatment of cytomegalovirus infection in immunocompetent hosts. http://www.uptodate.com/home. Accessed Dec. 12, 2013.

7. Cytomegalovirus (CMV) and congenital CMV infection: Transmission. Centers for Disease Control and Prevention. http://www.cdc.gov/cmv/transmission.html. Accessed Dec. 12, 2013.

8. Cytomegalovirus (CMV) and congenital CMV infection: Prevention. Centers for Disease Control and Prevention. http://www.cdc.gov/cmv/prevention.html. Accessed Dec. 12, 2013.

- HTLV virus
- CAT Scan
- Anita Baker
- Brenda Russell. God Bless You
- Susan Polis Schutz
- St. Augustine quote
- Albert Einstein
- Northern Dutchess Hospital in Rhinebeck
- Queen Elizabeth II once said, "Grief is the price we pay for love."
- Crocodile Dundee movie
- Adventures in Baby Sitting.
- Daniel Haughian poem titled: I Will Love You
- Hollywood Shuffle
- Sade Diamond Life Album
- Movie Jaws
- harmonic convergence

- Larry Levan
- 100 Black Men Coalition
- As 1987 came to a close 71,176 people are diagnosed with AIDS in the US, 41,027 are dead.
- St. Claire's Hospital New York City
- CNS toxoplasmosis
- Redding Funeral Home
- All is Fair in Love"Stevie Wonder
- AIDS Walk a thon
- Didn't we almost have it all-Whitney Houston
- Stevie Wonder –Rocket Love
- Never-Heart
- Gay Pride Week
- AIDS Memorial Quilt
- Robert Mapplethorp died of AIDS complications
- Life Spring
- 60 Year old Actress Amanda Blake died today
- At the end of 1990: 198,466 persons are diagnosed with AIDS in the US, 121,255 are dead.

www.ingramcontent.com/pod-product-compliance
Lightning Source LLC
Chambersburg PA
CBHW051536230426
43669CB00015B/2617